PRAISE FOR

The Ideal Life

"*The Ideal Life* brings together scientific insights, inspiring real-life stories of change, and carefully crafted tools and frameworks to help you live your life with a sense of purpose and joy. Mark's narration gives life and energy to scientific findings and human stories, and makes the reader feel the possibilities for regaining agency in their lives."

—**Ayse Yemiscigil, PhD**

Assistant Professor of Organizational Behavior, Gabelli School of Business at Fordham University; Research Affiliate, Human Flourishing Program at Harvard University; Research Fellow, International Humanistic Management Association

"Very inspiring book with simple steps that have impacted my life, my business, and not just reaching my goals, but finding more joy in the journey. Highly recommend it!"

—**Kirsten Wyatt**

Founder, Team Fit & Free; Wellness & Fitness Coach; Social Media Influencer

"The pursuit of happiness is an undeniable right to all humans. Wise men and women often say that happiness lies within, however, something has to be said for intentional goal setting. Goals and dreams are inspiring and energizing. Mark has developed a process that he came to call the I GOT This framework, helping himself and others achieve desirable results in all areas of life. *The Ideal Life* will help you understand how to apply the framework to make your life more meaningful and fulfilling."

—**Jana Peterkova Richter**
Former LPGA Tour Player, US Women's Open; Golf Instructor

"I'm so excited about this book—*The Ideal Life*! I'm an avid reader. I have never thought a book would truly change someone's life. This book will change lives! Who doesn't want to have purpose in their life? We all want a meaningful life. Mark has perfected a way to trigger the chemicals in our brain using the I GOT This framework to help us find meaning, to deal with stress and depression. All of this is important to help us to find Joy. Mark is real and the I GOT This framework has been proven to work. I hope you will invest in yourself by reading *The Ideal Life*, using the tools and applying the principles that Mark provides."

—**Bryan Beam**
Chief Operating Officer, Kellex Seating

"Mark provides an actionable and inspirational framework to live our most meaningful lives in all circumstances, backed by science. Looking forward to putting it in action!"

—**Muge Wood**
Global Energy Industry Solutions Delivery Lead, Microsoft; Member, Women's Energy Network of Houston and Greater Houston Partnership; Co-founder, "Refirement Life" podcast series; Board of Directors, "UTMA All Stars"

"I have observed that numerous individuals I know tend to postpone their retirement due to their uncertainty about how to discover their life's purpose. The Ideal Life framework offers practical guidance to assist individuals in taking concrete steps towards living a profoundly meaningful life, one that transcends short-term focus and embraces lasting significance."

—**Christine Zmuda**
Chief Inspiration Officer, Magnet Labs;
Co-Host of the "Refirement Life" Podcast

"Most of us have a general sense of our life's purpose but haven't done the work to clarify it or connect our daily decisions to align with that purpose. Mark's I GOT This Framework touches an emotional chord as it helps us fully unveil our purpose and then gives us the logical path to enable us to fully live into that purpose."

—**Jamie Tozzi**
Coach and Former Microsoft Executive

THE IDEAL LIFE

The Ideal Life

7 STEPS TO HARNESS YOUR STRESS,

DISCOVER YOUR PURPOSE,

AND **ACHIEVE YOUR GOALS**

Mark R.
Congdon

Forbes | Books

Published by Forbes Books, Charleston, South Carolina.
An imprint of Advantage Media Group.

Forbes Books is a registered trademark, and the Forbes Books colophon is a trademark of Forbes Media, LLC.

Printed in the United States of America.

10 9 8 7 6 5 4 3 2 1

ISBN: 979-8-88750-088-1 (Hardcover)
ISBN: 979-8-88750-089-8 (eBook)

Library of Congress Control Number: 2023921816

Cover and layout design by Matthew Morse.

Since 1917, Forbes has remained steadfast in its mission to serve as the defining voice of entrepreneurial capitalism. Forbes Books, launched in 2016 through a partnership with Advantage Media, furthers that aim by helping business and thought leaders bring their stories, passion, and knowledge to the forefront in custom books. Opinions expressed by Forbes Books authors are their own. To be considered for publication, please visit **books.Forbes.com**.

"Who has ever given to God, that God should repay them?"
For from Him and through Him and for Him are all things.
To Him be the glory forever! Amen.

—ROMANS 11:35–36

———

For Chelsea
10,958 × infinity
(that IS a lot)

———

To Lilly Grace, Addison, Caroline, and Parker
You GOT This!

Contents

From as early as I can remember, the crack of a bat and the feel of leather encompassing my hand in the backyard were pure joy. My love for baseball shaped my dreams and fueled my ambitions. Every goal I set for myself was driven by my vision of stepping onto the diamond one day as a professional baseball player.

The milestones I went on to achieve were reflections of my commitment. Right after high school I was drafted by the Pittsburgh Pirates in the thirty-first round. Ultimately I decided not to sign so that I could pursue an education at College of Charleston. While there, I continued my passion and played baseball for their team, the Cougars. As a junior, I was drafted once again, this time in the sixth round by the St. Louis Cardinals. After several seasons, I transitioned over to coaching, and in 2021 I embraced a new offer and became the youngest Major League Baseball manager in history by five years.

Looking back, I can confidently say that it wasn't just my love for the game that propelled me, but rather the unwavering discipline to chase a bigger picture that defined my journey and allowed me to become who I am today.

In the world of professional athletes, a singular focus often reigns supreme, leaving little room for distractions. Energy is channeled relentlessly toward excelling in the game, and doing everything humanly possible to advance to the next level. Priorities follow a pecking order as they are each ranked due to their relative importance to the sport—and one's life is ruled with this singular intention. When they are at the top of their game, life can feel thrilling, and it can remain at this level with ebbs and flows of pursuit and play, until it all suddenly changes.

Then, sadly, many athletes find themselves at a loss when thrown a curveball, or their career as they know it comes to an end. Some will pivot quickly and find joy in pursuing similar, or sometimes completely different, paths, but others will feel lost. When you have dedicated your entire life to one single goal, what happens after you achieve it? That question of "What comes next?" can feel utterly overwhelming to so many.

However, I consider myself fortunate as I discovered another truth years ago that allowed me to create a life worth living beyond the stadium—one that is fulfilling with equal measures of pride and passion, even though it is not played under the professional lights.

Now I am not just the Cardinals' manager; I am Amber's husband and a father to our precious daughter. We have built a foundation for our family that is rooted in faith, and together we have taken several short-term mission trips to orphanages across Central America. We have found purpose in giving back, helping others, and diving into our community.

The evolution of my baseball career continues to be inevitable, and while I hope to have many more years contributing to the sport I love, I can also look forward with a sense of peace. The knowledge that my journey is comprised of much more gives me confidence, reminding me that there's an abundance of joy yet to be experienced. My identity now stretches far beyond the boundaries of the ballpark.

These principles I live by resonate greatly with Mark's I GOT This framework, because it's not about achieving a single goal—as that is just a step along the way—but it is about the journey to discover your purpose, and to work toward something greater than yourself. It's about continuously pursuing a bigger picture.

This book embodies what I've long believed—that there are many areas of our life where we can find enjoyment, and that the pursuit of purpose across those multiple areas of your life will help you achieve your goals and find happiness.

My journey, and Mark's framework, are very similar. But what Mark's framework does, is provide you with a clear step by step guide that will assist you on your own path. So get ready to redefine your relationship with stress, and transform it into a driving force that propels you toward your dreams. Explore the seven life roles, and create a mission for each key area of your life. Enjoy inspiring stories of individuals who had to fight hard to get to where they are today, and explore the life lessons that they learned along the way.

I urge you to embark on this journey. Dive into the pages ahead to discover your purpose. Embrace the adventure and experience a fulfilling joyful life that is brighter than the stadium lights. You deserve it!

—**Oliver Marmol**
Professional Baseball Manager
St. Louis Cardinals Major League Baseball Team
As of the 2023 season, he is the youngest manager of any MLB team.

INTRODUCTION

"We want you to be happy."
—"JOY," PHISH

There is a lie that we all tell ourselves: *happiness can only come from achieving our goals and getting what we want.* This same voice that says that life is all about achievement also tells us which goals we should pursue. "You need more things," it says, "and *then* you will be happy. If only you had better looks and a bigger bank account, then all your problems would be solved."

The problem with this approach is that it doesn't work. In today's materialistic society, we have access to more stuff than any other time in history. Want this new iPhone? Just click here. How about that new car? There's financing for that. Not only do we have access to more things, we can get them faster than ever before. You might have bought this very book on Amazon and had it in your hands two days later. Or maybe you are listening to the audiobook, and it was only minutes ago that you were still thinking about whether you wanted to make your purchase.

If happiness was just about getting what we want, then the instant gratification of today's society should be creating access to a modern utopia. But instead, more stuff has only led to more stress.

Today, there is a higher rate of anxiety, depression, and suicide than any other time in history. People are turning to pills and other forms of medication in unprecedented numbers, but to a large extent, these drugs aren't solving the problem.

Chris Palmer, assistant professor of psychiatry at Harvard University and author of the book *Brain Energy*, recently told Dax Shepherd on his podcast *The Armchair Expert*:

> "Look around at the health and wellness of the human population. It is declining rapidly. Mental disorders are the leading cause of disability both in the United States and worldwide, with the single medical diagnosis of depression topping the list. Depression causes more people to not be able to work or go to school than any other medical illness on the planet. I think to most people that's shocking, because we have so many treatments for depression. We have dozens of antidepressants, we've got psychotherapy, we've got ketamine injections, we've got electroconvulsive therapy, and TMS, and *everything*, and a lot of people are getting those treatments, and they're not working."[1]

It's not just the desire for more stuff that leads us astray. There's also the lure of success that comes from seemingly healthy goals like getting a promotion or training for a triathlon. These goals might have positive outcomes, but they are short-lived. Achieving our goals—in our finances, our health, or even our relationships—may give us satisfaction in the short term, but that feeling is never permanent.

I have had my own share of success, and I can tell you firsthand that none of my achievements has ever made my stress disappear. In fact, despite those successes, I have still struggled my whole life with anxiety and depression. Even today, I suffer from panic attacks that severely disrupt my ability to function and leave me struggling for days afterward.

The feelings associated with these attacks begin as a sudden rapid heartbeat, immediately followed by a warmth that flows from my chest into my arms and down into my legs. That feeling is then followed by a prickly sensation on my skin that kind of feels like goosebumps, except that my hairs don't actually stick up. I'm not always aware of what triggers these attacks, but it is obvious that there is a chemical cocktail flowing throughout my body and causing all kinds of different thoughts and feelings. For minutes afterward, and even sometimes for an hour or longer, my mind is basically useless, hijacked by an inner monologue that always seems to hinge on one main theme: *What do I do next?*

When this happens, I feel lost—all alone, and with no path forward. I've tried all sorts of ways to cope with my anxiety. For a while, I turned to external sources for chemical satisfaction when my major life goals didn't bring me the lasting happiness I was looking for. I have tried prescription anxiety medications, but primarily I self-medicated with alcohol, cigarettes, and junk food. In each case, the immediate escape these outlets provided was always replaced by the same anxiety that had been waiting for me just around the corner.

I may experience anxiety more acutely than the average person, but I know from coaching others through their own challenges that most people routinely feel some version of this inner turmoil. Whether it's going through a midlife crisis or just trying to make it through another day, we are all haunted by that same question: *What's next?*

The Stress of What's Next

When I was ten years old, my family went on a Spring Break ski vacation to Vermont. It was the end of a long day on the slopes, and we were all tired. Earlier that day, my parents had bought me a brand-new ski suit as a reward for how well I had been doing. It was a bright red one-piece, and I felt like an Olympic athlete when I wore it. Slope after slope, I tucked my body and flew recklessly down the hill, testing my skills and seeing how fast I could pass by the other skiers. At the end of the day, when my parents said they were exhausted and eager to get back to the hotel room, I pleaded for just one more run.

As I started down the final slope, a cloud settled onto the mountain and obscured my vision. The late afternoon snow had become icy, and I had trouble navigating the moguls as I began working my way down the mountain. About halfway down, I slid on a patch of ice and rocketed off the side of the mountain, hitting one tree, and then another. Luckily the second tree stopped me about ten feet short from falling down a fifty-foot cliff, but it also fractured my femur, which came just millimeters from hitting my femoral artery.

My brother, Whit, was with me and flagged down help, and paramedics brought me down the mountain on a snowmobile. I don't remember any pain, probably because my body immediately went into shock. The only thing I remember clearly was the doctors cutting that bright red ski suit off of my leg, and feeling like I had let my parents down. After several surgeries, the doctors set my leg with an external fixator—a cruel contraption that included four large metal bars that stuck completely out of my leg, with another bar that held them all together outside my body.

My first year of middle school was spent in a wheelchair. Sometimes I felt like this actually helped me make friends, as classmates took turns giving me wheelies and racing me down the hall. But other times it made me wonder who my friends really were. A particularly traumatic memory came when I was being given a wheelie on the playground blacktop, when the chair tipped over and spilled me out onto the ground, the fixator sticking out of my leg and into the air. Scared that they would get in trouble, everyone scattered—leaving me alone on the hot black tar, crawling to get back to my wheelchair and climb my way back in. That's my earliest memory of feeling alone.

Another tough memory came that summer, when a couple of friends rode their bikes over to my house to visit with me. We had as good of a time as ten-year-old boys can have when stuck inside on a warm summer day, but eventually they said their goodbyes and headed back outside to explore the creek that ran through our neighborhood. As I sat by myself next to the window of the empty playroom and watched as they pedaled out of my driveway, I again felt completely alone, and I cried.

For the next year it felt like life was passing me by while I sat in that wheelchair feeling sorry for myself. I know now that these memories contributed to the source of social angst that I continue to carry with me today. *Will I be left alone again?* I often wonder. *Does anyone actually like me? What's to like, anyway?*

Unable to answer these questions in the moment, I turned to the future for hope. Once I get older, I thought, all of this will make sense. I began to set my sights on major milestones that I could look forward to. First, it was the freedom of getting my driver's license that gave me hope. *As soon as I can get out of the house,* I thought, *then I won't have to sit around by myself anymore.*

And indeed, getting my driver's license felt great—for a time. I will always remember the joy that I felt on my first solo drive down a two-lane country road in Goochland, Virginia, listening to "Freebird" blast from the speakers. But as the days went by, my life didn't experience the sudden change that I had been hoping for. On Friday nights, when I knew there had to be some party going on nearby that I wasn't invited to, I used to drive for hours around those same country roads pretending like I had somewhere to go, only to realize that I had been driving in circles.

So, I set my sights even further down the road. *Once I go to college*, I said to myself, *then I will figure out what I am doing with my life.* And again, I experienced some short-term relief when I realized that goal and moved into my dorm at Clemson University. I made new friends, joined a fraternity, and finally took part in the social experiences that I thought would fill the void in my life. But no matter how much fun I thought I was having at the time, my worries were always waiting for me.

A lot of my anxious thoughts at that time focused on money. The little income I earned from waiting tables went straight to the alcohol that I hoped would take my mind off my stress. On more than one occasion I had to hunt for coins in the cracks of my car seats just to fill my gas tank enough to make it to campus. The worry of running out of money fueled the rest of my concerns, and I spiraled down into depression.

When I get a real job, I thought, then *I will have the financial security to figure things out, and maybe then I'll be happy.*

You can see the pattern here. When getting a job didn't solve everything, then it was getting married, then having kids, then switching jobs to something I really cared about, and on and on. The focal point of my worry always seemed to pivot from one thing to another, but the theme was always the same: *What's next?*

The temptation for me to believe that lasting happiness is still just around the corner has continued even into today. Right now the next big milestone is finishing this book (which is ironically about helping other people control their own anxiety) Once it is published, I will have finally accomplished my dream to be a writer, and then I'll definitely be happy. *Right?*

You Can Harness Your Stress

Luckily, I don't believe that lie anymore. Now don't get me wrong, each one of the milestones that I have looked forward to in life has made me happy in the moment, and my wife and kids especially have been sustainable sources of joy. But the truth is that my stress remains. That's because I'm human, and humans are designed to feel stress. Our species evolved into an environment where threats to our survival were a part of daily life, and it was the extra vigilance and awareness of our ancestor's fight-or-flight response that kept them alive. By always thinking about "what's next," they were better prepared for potential threats that might arise.

The fact that we regularly experience stress is not the problem—our bodies are made for that. The problem is that our modern minds often can't make sense of how that stressful energy is serving a purpose. For our early ancestors, that purpose was survival. These same survival instincts are still triggered today, but we aren't usually faced with a physical enemy to fight or predator to flee. All of the chemicals that are released to get our muscles moving are instead left to linger in our bloodstream, resulting in meaningless anxiety and a wide range of negative impacts to our health.

Fortunately, we can learn to harness our stress and repurpose it toward an even greater meaning than that of our evolutionary design. In this book, you will learn how the psychology of your mind can empower you to not just survive but to thrive. Over the past fifteen years, I have been able to stop my slide into depression and steadily work my way back to a life full of joy. My stress still remains, but more often than not I am able to control it and use it for my own benefit. Rather than waiting for what's next, I now *decide* what's next by focusing on the things in my life that I can control, and aligning my goals with a fixed vision of the person that I want to become. This has required a total shift in mindset, which I have been able to achieve through the development of a framework centered around the concept of what I refer to as a personal *Ideal*.

When You Begin with the End in Mind

The seed for this framework was planted in my mind by a book. I remember it clearly: it was 2009, and I was sitting on my friend's couch in his Clemson apartment, where a group of us had gotten together for a pre-graduation party. On the coffee table next to me, I noticed a worn-down book with a red and white cover. For no particular reason, I decided to pick it up and start reading. The title of the book was *The 7 Habits of Highly Effective People* written by Stephen R. Covey, and I was instantly captivated.

Inside, Covey started by saying that we all have a "best version of ourselves," one that we can identify with and move toward if we just take the time to listen to our inner voice. He went on to describe specific tools and exercises that would help identify that ideal self, and then explained how we can turn that vision into a reality by increasing the amount of control we exert in our life. By starting with the end in mind and then connecting that destination all the way back to the next step forward, we can move incrementally closer to being the type of person that we wish to become, and it is this forward progress that leads to lasting happiness.[2]

Reading this message, I could not help but feel like I was holding a treasure map in my hands, one that would guide me out of my misery and toward a more joyful life. A life that I could control, rather than being at the mercy of my environment. Up to that point I had felt like I was drifting, without any particular direction. Now, I felt like I could figure out how to move forward, and that epiphany ended up making all the difference. Just the *idea* of a brighter future was enough to make my current life seem better.

I put the book down and realized that it was dark outside and that everyone was gone. As I became fully absorbed in what I was reading, I had lost all track of time and had apparently told everyone to head to the bars without me. In hindsight, I now know that I had experienced a state of *flow* (more to come on that later), but, in the moment, I just knew that I had reached a turning point in my life. I thought about heading out to meet up with my friends, but then sat down and picked the book back up. I had work to do.

A Path to Purpose

The year after discovering Covey's *7 Habits* and graduating from Clemson, I sold my car and moved to Charleston, South Carolina. With barely enough money to cover my rent, I took a minimum-wage job as a valet at a downtown parking garage until eventually landing an entry-level position in the transportation logistics industry. Then, I got busy implementing a new plan to align my goals in a way that placed a priority on consistently becoming more like an ideal future version of myself, rather than on the achievement of short-term milestones that had been dominating my mind to that point.

Despite de-emphasizing my immediate goals and focusing on a longer-term vision, this new mindset actually ended up helping me to achieve higher levels of short-term success than I ever had before. Over the next few years I earned one promotion after another, eventually landing a role as the vice president of operations at an international shipping association—a job that involved flying across the globe and single-handedly negotiating multimillion-dollar contracts with top executives of international steamship lines.

I was still in my mid-twenties and had already climbed my way into a six-figure salary and a position of influence within my industry. But more importantly, I was feeling fulfilled by my success instead of being manipulated by it. I still dealt with stress, but I used that chaotic energy to create inner order through the pursuit of difficult but meaningful goals. In this way, my new mental framework had helped me to convert my anxiety from a crutch into a crucible, like the ones that medieval alchemists used in their attempts to change lead into gold. It wasn't a cure for my pain, but with my "Ideal Life" in mind, I knew that I was moving in the right direction.

Empowered by this success, I decided to leave the international logistics industry and join my brother Whit in starting a trucking company in 2018. As President, I supported Whit's knowledge of running a trucking company by applying the concept of the Ideal toward the development of our firm's overarching mission and culture, and used it to develop relationships with our external vendors and customers. Again, the success was immediate and impactful: in less than two years, we had grown to millions in revenue, operations in seven states, and over fifty employees.

Over the ten years it took to get from parking cars to company president, I was able to grow the seed of my new mindset into a fully developed process that I eventually came to call the I GOT This framework, which is an acronym for Ideal, Goals, Objectives, and Tasks. It begins with a best-case, future scenario of an Ideal Life, and then backs into the present through a carefully crafted sequence of goal setting. By breaking the framework down into seven simple steps that can be repeated over and over again (which you will learn about over the course of this book), I was able to consistently apply this framework and experience sustainable results.

The Seven Steps of the I GOT This Framework

STEP 1 **I**deal

STEP 2
STEP 3 **G**oals ⟨ DREAM GOALS
STEP 4 HORIZON GOALS
MILESTONE GOALS

STEP 5 **O**bjectives

STEP 6 **T**asks

STEP 7 **THIS**

I crafted this framework within my career, but I soon began applying it to other areas of my life, beginning with my health. Since high school I had steadily gained 5–10 pounds every year, and by 2015 I weighed over 235 pounds with hardly any muscle. I was totally sedentary, smoked a pack of cigarettes a day, and drank regularly to cope with my constant anxiety. My body was only twenty-eight years old, but it was already starting to break down. When I threw my back out while bending over to change my daughter's diaper, I knew something had to change.

I'll tell the story of exactly how I applied the I GOT This framework to my health later in this book, but here are the highlights. In the first year I lost over 60 pounds. In year two, I lost another 20 pounds and ran my first marathon, and in year three I completed a full Ironman Triathlon: a 2.4-mile swim, followed by a 112-mile bike race, followed by a 26.2-mile run—back-to-back-to-back!

For my entire life, I had struggled with failed diets and half-hearted exercise plans, only to fall off the wagon and end up worse than when I started. But when I applied the steps of the I GOT This framework, I was able to maintain the consistency needed to stay on track. And the best part was that as much as I enjoyed those successful outcomes, I began to feel the joy of the framework the first day I began intentionally pursuing the long-term vision of my personal Ideal.

After my weight loss journey, I began applying the I GOT This framework to other areas of my life and experienced the same positive outcomes in all of them. I was able to fully eliminate $20,000 in debt, work through challenges in my family relationships until they were stronger than ever before, and even establish a renewed discipline in my personal faith.

Eventually I came to realize that there was something about this framework that made it nearly foolproof—but what really got me excited was when I started seeing the results that it had for others.

The Power of Purpose

As I shared my personal experiences with people, they began asking me how they could use the I GOT This framework in their own lives—so I developed a step-by-step guide and began coaching individuals through the process. The results were astounding. I helped one person achieve break-out sales in his new position within the cyber-security industry. Another was able to use the framework to develop a walking routine that unlocked a motivation for her to start working out again for the first time in years. A sales manager at an international pharmaceutical company utilized the program with his team, and in less than six months his group went from last to first place in national sales, with higher levels of employee engagement and lower levels of turnover than the manager had ever seen before.

One person after another reported that the I GOT This framework was unlocking a renewed joy in their life and leading them to positive outcomes in every pursuit they applied it to. What convinced me to leave the logistics industry and begin sharing this framework with people full time, though, was the way my mom, Kay Congdon, used it in her fight against cancer. In 2020, Kay was diagnosed with Stage 4 breast cancer, which had spread into her ribcage, many of her lymph nodes (including an egg-sized one directly behind her sternum), her sternum itself, her pelvic bones, her femur, two of her vertebrae, and even into her skull. Her doctors started her on treatments, but they still only gave her a few months to live. During that time, Kay committed herself to using the I GOT This framework as a way to unlock as much joy as she could in the remaining days of her life.

But then something incredible happened—the cancer began to disappear. Within a month of implementing the framework, her tumors had shrunk to nearly half their original size. A month after that, they had dropped in half again. By the time the doctors had thought that Kay would be dead, her blood results were indicating that she may live for many years to come.

That was three years ago from the time I am writing this, and as of today she is still going strong. The medicine that she was taking certainly impacted her recovery, but the doctors who prescribed those drugs still said that the results were "miraculous" and the hospital even created a documentary about her story. Clearly there was something going on inside her body that had created an environment where the medicine could better do its job, and Kay believed that it was the mindset of the I GOT This framework that had done the trick.

After seeing these results I made the decision to leave the logistics industry and start The Ideal Life, a company with a mission to help people experience the same type of positive outcomes that I have seen in myself and others. I also enrolled in a master's program at Harvard's Extension School in Industrial-Organizational Psychology (the psychology of individuals and how they interact in teams) and learned the amazing impact that our mindset can have on the chemical makeup of our brains and bodies. This knowledge helped to explain why my mom's intense stress had likely facilitated the growth of her cancer in the first place, and how her refreshed "I GOT This" mindset had unlocked a healthier internal environment. It also explained similar results that the coaches in my company began to witness with the people they worked with, such as one client who in less than a year of using the I GOT This framework saw his blood sugars improve to the point where his doctors reduced the amount of diabetes medication he was required to take.

Let me be clear—I am not a medical doctor (or a doctor of any kind), and I also firmly believe that medicine, when prescribed by a competent professional, is a critical component to managing and recovering from illness. At the same time, I also know that mindset is also a medicine, and that we have way more control over our inner design than most of us give ourselves credit for. The choices we make about how we think and act can have a direct impact on the development of diseases and the extent to which they can be treated.

You GOT This

The I GOT This framework is based on the fundamental facts of our human design, which was established during the evolution of our species. Over the past decade, I have consolidated the lessons that I've learned in trying to better understand the human brain and body into a framework that reflects the philosophy of a growth mindset. Over those years, I've devoted myself to the study of human psychology and how to apply the latest scientific findings to the development of practices that can be used in daily life. I have also accumulated stories from top performers who have been able to achieve fulfilling happiness in their own life, both through personal conversations and interviews as well as through the research of historical figures. Finally, all of these lessons have been integrated into coaching practices that I've used to help both individuals and teams achieve positive outcomes in a wide variety of contexts.

Throughout my studies at Harvard, my research for this book, and my experiences coaching people and teams at The Ideal Life, a common theme has emerged that I have woven into the principles originally established by the successes of my own career. This theme is captured within the seven simple steps of "I GOT This," which is both a framework and a philosophy. Its core elements can be seen in the life of virtually any fulfilled, joyful individual, regardless of what words they use to describe their own personal process. The odds are that you are already implementing many of these steps in your personal life, but just thinking about them in different terminology.

My aim for this book is for you to feel reinforced in the healthy habits you are already implementing, while also learning some new ideas that you can carry with you into the rest of your life. I believe that anyone who makes the decision to implement the ideas behind the seven steps of the I GOT This framework will be able to harness their stress, discover their purpose, and achieve their goals—with two caveats.

The first is that your main focus in implementing these steps can never be just about achieving your goals. As I will explain throughout this book, happiness does not come primarily from goal achievement, but rather goal *pursuit*. Our major goals serve us best when they are aligned with both the short-term actions required to succeed, as well as the long-term impact that they will have on our lives. When we place too much focus on the outcomes of the goals themselves, we lose this alignment. Not only do we not connect to our sense of purpose, but we lose sight of what actions we should be taking next.

The second critical component to the success of the I GOT This framework is that you must be willing to consistently push yourself out of your comfort zone and have the perseverance to return to that discomfort over and over again. This is not a "get happy quick" plan that promises an end to all of your struggles. Indeed, a certain amount of stress is required for goal pursuit, and you must learn to embrace that pain as much as the pleasure that comes with goal achievement. It is the consistent application of pressure toward the pursuit of purpose that leads to joy in the present moment.

If you are OK with those conditions, then let's begin. My hope for this book is that it plants a seed in the lives of readers, just like Covey's words inspired my own journey so many years ago. If it can help one person learn how to navigate their own personal path toward purpose, then it has been a success. I hope it helps *you*.

You are the hero of your journey, and this book can be your guide. So if you are up for it, let's begin. You GOT This!

CHAPTER 1

Into the Ideal

Creating Order out of Chaos

> "The order in the chaos
> waits to be perceived."
>
> —"MERCURY," PHISH

Since the beginning of recorded history, humans have been trying to figure out what life is all about. Aristotle, one of the biggest influencers in the history of Western thought, claimed the answer was to be happy. "Happiness is the meaning and purpose of life," Aristotle said, and "the whole aim and end of human existence."[1]

Even if we think we are doing something for someone else's well-being, Aristotle proposed, those actions can always be tied back to our own personal desire for happiness. For example, I want to provide for my children so that *they* grow up to be happy, but ultimately, I can't deny that this outcome would then lead to my own positive feelings. The same thing can be said for charitable giving or volunteer work. No matter what we *think* our motives are, Aristotle said, the outcomes of our actions can always be traced back to our own internal emotions, whether we are fully conscious of it or not.

For Aristotle, though, happiness didn't mean feeling constant pleasure or even being comfortable all the time. The Greek word that he used to describe this feeling was *eudaimonia*, which is actually better translated as "well-being." For him, this sense of general fulfillment that has been translated as happiness was a constantly moving target that included both the pleasure *and the pain* of a purpose-driven life.

In this chapter, I'll set the stage for the seven steps of the I GOT This framework by providing an argument for how stress can be harnessed to create happiness and why this process inevitably leads to joy.

You Can Find Joy in Suffering

To say that life is all about being happy would be ignoring the painful periods of life that allow for positive outcomes to occur. There are times in life when feeling pain is inevitable, and even necessary. It is natural to grieve the loss of a loved one, for example, and this is in fact critical to the coping process. Indeed, we could not fully appreciate our worldly relationships in the first place without the realization that they are only temporary. A similar, yet less extreme, example is the discomfort that arises in the pursuit of physical or mental skill development. Anyone who has trained for a sport or studied for an exam knows that progress doesn't come easy. If we only desired to feel good all the time, we wouldn't have our innate desire for self-improvement. Dr. Shelly Carson, a professor of psychology at Harvard, put it to me this way: "If the only thing that matters is happiness, then we would just give everyone cocaine."

Rather than happiness, I think a more appropriate word to capture what Aristotle meant by *eudaimonia* would be "joy," which I define as the energy released by balancing both pleasure and pain in the pursuit of purpose. Happiness is a component of joy, but so is stress. In fact, joy can be achieved even in the most difficult of situations, as long as some form of meaning can be attributed to the experience.

The complex feelings associated with joy are generated by a surprisingly small number of chemicals that blend together like a color wheel to create all of the emotions of the human experience. There are four primary hormones associated with the feelings of pleasure, which can be easily remembered by the acronym DOSE: dopamine, oxytocin, serotonin, and endorphins. These chemicals are released to reward us for both the pursuit and achievement of goals and make us feel motivated, connected, fulfilled, and blissful. On the other side of the equation is cortisol, which manages our stress response. Cortisol can give us a boost of focused energy when it is controlled, but is also the source of chronic anxiety when allowed to run rampant.

The DOSE of Happiness

HORMONES ⟶ HAPPINESS

Dopamine ⟶ Motivated

Oxytocin ⟶ Connected

Serotonin ⟶ Fulfilled

Endorphins → Blissful

Joyful living involves being aware of life's emotions, both the pleasure and the pain, and learning how to balance the chemicals of our internal design by connecting both the high times and the low to the same focal point of purpose. When we concentrate on just the good, or just the bad, we are distracted from our core mission in life and lose our opportunity to experience joy. Happiness ebbs and flows, but joy is sustainable as long as we are able to identify a goal for our life and keep that vision in front of us.

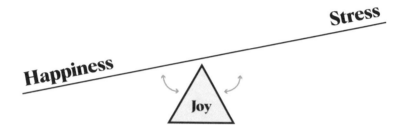

The Value of Order

The reason why a focus on purpose can generate joy is because of the way goals help our brains make sense of life. The world is a chaotic place, and our brains do not like chaos. Chaos is unpredictable, and therefore dangerous, and so our brains are constantly on the lookout for how to create order within the uncertainty of our external environment. They do this by establishing a hierarchy of goals and aligning them into one centralized structure of meaning.

To appreciate how much the brain values order, just look around you. Nature displays a pattern of order in virtually everything you see, and the more organized and complex that order is, the more beautiful it appears to the human eye. Take the natural element of carbon, for example, which is the building block of all organic life. Pure carbon in its most unorganized form appears as coal—a black, lumpy material that shows up in our stocking after a year spent making our parents' house particularly messy. Arrange that same carbon in patterned layers, however, and it becomes graphite—a gray material that we can mold and sharpen, and use in pencils to write our parents a Christmas card that totally erases any memory of messy behavior.

But the real magic occurs when those same layers are spread evenly apart so that every carbon atom is exactly the same distance from each other, resulting in a beautiful diamond that gets Dad off cleaning duty when it is placed under the Christmas tree in a box with Mom's name written on it. A diamond has significantly higher value than graphite, which likewise has a higher value than coal. It's the same element—it just has more order!

Everywhere we look, there are precise patterns in nature that demonstrate amazing order. Whether it's the blooming of flower petals in precise Fibonacci sequences, the "golden ratio" of a human face that maximizes attractiveness to a potential partner, or the fractals that form a snowflake, there is an attraction to these patterns that captivates our attention.

Goals Are How Our Brains Create Order

Internally, the brain creates its own order out of the chaos of its environment by looking at all incoming information through the lens of our goals. Throughout the day, our senses are bombarded by thousands of inputs that the brain must quickly compute. When we can quickly filter out the things that don't matter, then we can make better decisions about what to do next. We do this through an internal hierarchy of goals, at the top of which is an ideal outcome for our life that represents the type of person we wish to become.

This internal organization of goals is not just there to guide you—in a very real sense, it is the way in which you identify who you are as a person. Mihaly Csikszentmihalyi (pronounced MEE-high Cheek-SENT-mee-high), the late Hungarian-American psychologist whose expertise was in human happiness, argued that "more than anything else, the self represents the hierarchy of goals that we have built up, bit by bit, over the years."[2] The better we can consciously identify our own hierarchy of goals, and especially the ultimate goal that we have for our life, the better chance we have at understanding who we are and who we want to be. We all have an idea of the person we want to become, whether we are consciously aware of it or not, and aligning with that vision is our brain's top priority.

Angela Duckworth, a leading expert in the field of positive psychology, calls this top goal the mind's "ultimate concern," and describes it as a navigational tool that guides all our thoughts and actions. It's important to identify a single ultimate concern, she warns: "You need *one* internal compass, not two, three, four or five."[3] This is important advice, because we all play many different roles in life and they can compete for our attention and spread us thin. When we can connect these areas of our life to one comprehensive goal, however, they begin to work together.

In the I GOT This framework, the Ideal represents this top-level goal. The Goals, Objectives, and Tasks of the framework represent the long-, medium-, and short-term goals that can be connected to the Ideal through a step-by-step process designed to establish alignment and create the inner order that your brain craves. Each of the following chapters in this book is dedicated to one of the framework's seven steps that lead to this alignment. When pieced together, the elements of this framework create a path toward purpose that, when followed, unlocks the joy of our brain's inner reward system.

Creating Order out of Chaos

It's not enough just to identify your goals—you must also actively pursue them in order to unlock the joy that comes with knowing you are on the right path. Life is constantly throwing more chaos our way, and if we can't connect new experiences to an existing hierarchy of goals, then that chaos will overwhelm us. That's why even more than order itself, our brains are especially attracted to the *creation* of order out of chaos.

For example, think about how good it feels to have cleaned a cluttered house. With four little kids running around, Chelsea and I are usually too tired to do this ourselves, but we love watching TV shows about other people getting organized. In 2019, Marie Kondo took the world by storm with a Netflix special about home organization called *Tidying Up with Marie Kondo,* in which she visited the homes of American families and applied her unique "KonMari" method to help them declutter their living environments. Based on the Japanese Shinto religion, the KonMari method places a priority on the person rather than on their possessions. Believing that a proper order to the things in our lives will lead to an increased sense of energy and alignment, Marie Kondo directs her clients to throw away anything in their home that doesn't "spark joy."

As part of her process, Kondo enters a home as if she were approaching a Shinto shrine, speaking to the house directly. As she explains it, "The first thing I do when I visit a client is to greet their home. I kneel formally on the floor in the center of the house—or where its vortex is—and address the home in my mind … after introducing myself—including my name and occupation—I ask for help in creating a space where its inhabitants can enjoy a happier life."[4]

Kondo's eccentric approach to the importance of organization and order in life sparked a wave of amusing internet memes, but it also generated significant attention to the merit of her framework itself. In only a few years after writing *The Life-Changing Magic of Tidying Up: The Japanese Art of Decluttering and Organizing*, Kondo's books had already sold over ten million copies in forty countries. Kondo's message resonates because it works. Behind her rituals and heartfelt conversations with inanimate objects, there really is a life-changing magic in the solution she offers to her clients. But where does this magic come from?

Her process itself is not ground-breaking, nor is it based on any type of scientific evidence about the most strategic way to organize. Essentially, it simply involves going through a client's house and making a big pile of one category at a time, such as shoes, clothing, or photographs, and throwing out any items that don't "spark joy." Then, the homeowner puts the remaining items back in an appropriate place. It sounds like common sense, but it has an extraordinary effect on her clients, who are always overcome with emotion when they enter their newly ordered living spaces.

The magic behind Kondo's approach comes from the fact that she places her focus on the *feeling* that her clients get when they prioritize the things that matter the most to them. When they organize and establish order out of this meaning, a spark of joy is ignited within them that speaks directly to their soul. There is just something about getting organized that recharges the spirit.

The Magic of Music

Personally, my favorite way to appreciate the creation of order out of chaos is by listening to music. At any given point in time, our eardrums are being bombarded with air molecules. Music is able to manipulate those molecules into specific wavelengths that sound pleasing to the ears because of the way they fit into a specific order of rules that we call harmony. If the notes violate those rules, they just sound like noise, which bothers us. But when we hear well-played music, we love it. Music doesn't just sound pleasing—it has real physical benefits as well. Studies show that music can reduce anxiety, lower blood pressure, and even improve sleep.

These benefits are a big reason why music has always been an integral part of human culture. Learning to play an instrument is difficult and takes years of training, which is why we value talented musicians so much. But even more difficult is the ability to create new music on the fly, which is the essence of jazz and its modern counterpart, the "jam band."

The jam band Phish is my all-time favorite group because of their incredible ability to convert the chaos of dissonant noise into the harmony of blissful music in front of a live audience. In the middle of a song, one band member will begin "jamming" by introducing a different chord or key, which will temporarily disrupt the collective harmony of the group, resulting in dissonance that would normally be unpleasant to an audience. But by carefully listening and making their own adjustments, the other members of the band realign with that rogue musician until the group reestablishes order, once again achieving harmony and playing the song in a way that they have never done before. Having attended many of their shows, the only word I can use to describe this experience is *joyful.*

You will notice that each chapter of this book begins with a Phish song lyric. This is not just me being a fan but also a reminder that each step of the I GOT This framework is designed to help you create order out of the chaos in your life by connecting your actions to an established goal hierarchy organized around the vision of The

Ideal Life. This process aligns with the rules of our inner design, and the harmony that results from that alignment unlocks the chemicals that make us feel joyful.

Every day we are faced with a limitless choice of actions to take, with each one leading to a number of potential outcomes. When we don't have a clear sense of our self (i.e., our goals), the chaos of those choices can overwhelm us. But when we have done the work to plan a clear path forward, we can choose to act in ways that align with a purposeful goal. When we do this, we unlock the joyful energy of our inner reward system.

The Chaordic Funnel of Our Soul

By converting chaos into order, the human goal-setting system is an example of what Nobel Prize–winning chemist Ilya Prigogine called *dissipative structures*: "physical systems that harness energy which otherwise would be dispersed and lost in random motion."[5] Humans have leveraged such systems throughout history, all the way from the invention of fire—which takes the potential energy stored in a fuel source like wood and converts it into heat that can cook food—to the steam engine, which uses that heat to create mechanical energy that transports people and goods around the world.

The human brain is a dissipative structure because it converts the chaos of potential choices into the order of structured goals. It is capable of harnessing the same stress that causes anxiety and using that energy to accomplish the things that are most important to us, and in doing so it unlocks the joy of knowing that we are on the right path in life. I refer to this process as a *chaordic funnel*, because it works by translating the chaos of *what's next* into the structured order of short-term goals that can be acted upon in the present moment.

Chaordic Funnels Unlock Potential Energy
by Converting Chaos into Order

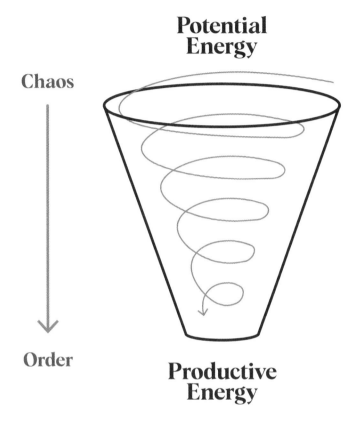

The I GOT This framework facilitates this chaordic process by aligning the distant, abstract vision of the Ideal with immediate Tasks, and in doing so unlocks the motivating energy of our inner reward system. It does this through a systematic, step-by-step process that converts the chaos of choice into the order of action. It begins with identifying the Ideal (Step 1). Then, you connect that vision with a sequence of long-, medium-, and short-term outcomes that would demonstrate progress on the path toward that end goal. These outcomes are represented by the Dream Goal (Step 2), the Horizon Goal (Step 3), and the Milestone Goal (Step 4). Next, you select a set of controllable Objectives (Step 5) and complement them with an identity-based habit to work on through daily Tasks (Step 6). As you work your way through the framework, the productive energy that is unlocked by this process spills over into every other area of your life. All of a sudden you will notice that you are able to confront the challenges in your life with a joyful mindset that says, "I GOT This" (Step 7).

The Chaordic Funnel of the I GOT This Framework

Over the past fifteen years, I have refined this seven-step process using the practical experiences of my career and coaching and pairing them with the lessons learned in Harvard psychology classrooms, creating a robust program that anyone can use to take back control over their life. During that time, I have noticed the principles of this framework at work in the stories of the successful individuals and teams that I have spoken with and studied. They don't use the same words for their process, and most of them don't have a systematic way to describe it. But there is a common thread in every story: the deliberate pursuit of an identity-based goal through controllable actions that consistently push them out of our comfort zone. This is the essence of a growth mindset, and the more any of us can implement such an approach in our daily life, the more our internal chemistry will reward us for establishing more order in our lives. The I GOT This framework is designed to facilitate such a mindset.

In this book, I will talk about this philosophy of growth using the framework and terminology of I GOT This, but it will not be a step-by-step "How-To Guide" of how to specifically implement this framework. Rather, it will be a "Why It Works Guide" that will give you the information and examples needed for you to apply its lessons in your own life, however you choose to identify with it. To help you translate these ideas into action, I have included some reflection questions at the end of each chapter. If you are interested in a complete step-by-step guide to the I GOT This framework, you can use the QR code at the end of this chapter to access additional coaching resources.

One Path to Purpose

Before we get started, one more word of warning: as you begin to see the positive effects of the I GOT This framework, you will be tempted to apply it to all areas of your life at once. Don't do that. The deliberate practice required by the pursuit of purpose is difficult. After all, if creating diamonds out of coal was easy, they wouldn't be so valuable. When we get out of our comfort zone in too many areas at the same time, we run the risk of burnout. I've been through this several times myself, and it's not good. It's tempting to think you can accomplish more at a faster pace, but you'll end up halting your progress altogether. Besides, the point of the framework itself is not to reach a destination but to pursue it.

The good news is that the energy that the framework unlocks affects your other life roles, anyway, and so you will notice progress being made in those areas even without additional effort. The real keys to maximizing the effectiveness of the framework are consistency and coaching. This book can help with the latter. Now, let's get started with Step 1: Identify Your Master Goal.

The ◆ Ideal

Step 1: Identify Your Master Goal

Stress

| Dream Goal |
| Horizon Goal |
| Milestone Goal |
| Objectives |
| Tasks |

Joy

This

Step 2: Visualize (But Don't Fantasize)

Step 3: Outline the Story of Your Life

Step 4: Find the Sweet Spot of Success

Step 5: Control the Controllables

Step 6: Make Happiness a Habit

Step 7: Deliberately Flow

CHAPTER 2

Step 1: Identify Your Master Goal

The Ideal

"You try to see your future from the line."

—"THE LINE," PHISH

My wife Chelsea and I have three little girls (Lilly Grace, Addison, and Caroline) and a baby boy (Parker), so of course we love Disney World. During our most recent Spring Break, we experienced one of our best visits yet to the most magical place on earth. We did it all—Magic Kingdom, of course, but also Animal Kingdom, Hollywood Studios, and Epcot. We even snuck away from Mickey for a day and hit up Volcano Bay, the water park at Universal Studios. During the trip, we celebrated Addison's sixth birthday, and Parker took his first steps. There was nonstop action, we did things we had never done before, and everyone was happy.

Then, we got home, and that elated feeling seemed to disappear as soon as we walked in the door. The house felt empty and even a little dark, even though it was a bright sunny day. Something just felt off, and we couldn't quite put our finger on it. But I knew what had happened—it was the dreaded postvacation blues.

Odds are this has happened to you, as well. Whenever humans experience something really great, like a vacation or accomplishing a major goal, there is often a comedown that overshadows the positive mood that we just experienced. The reason for this is due to dopamine, the DOSE chemical responsible for making us feel so good in the first place. Dopamine is released to reward us when we achieve something important or experience something new. When our goals are really big or we do a lot of novel things in a short period of time (like my family's Disney trip), our brains get flooded with a rush of dopamine. But once those rewards are received, the dopamine stops flowing, and we feel the negative effects of that crash.

When we place all of our focus on goal achievements or major life milestones, we risk falling into this dopamine trap. The bigger the reward, the bigger the potential for a letdown. For example, consider the story of Michael Phelps, who accomplished one of the greatest feats in human history—and paid the price.

The Weight of Gold

Over the course of his career, Phelps rose to the highest level of swimming achievement, becoming the most decorated Olympian in history and winning more gold medals (twenty-three) than the combined count of over 170 *countries*. Indeed, many consider him to be the greatest athlete of all time, but he didn't start out that way. When Phelps first began swimming at age seven, it was mainly because his older sisters were already on a team and his parents wanted to simplify the carpool process. But like his siblings, Phelps quickly fell in love with the sport and started to develop a purpose in the way he practiced. Over time, he became one of the best swimmers of his generation.

In the 2004 Summer Games in Athens, Phelps had a breakthrough performance that resulted in eight total medals (six gold and two bronze)—the second-best performance ever behind the all-time great swimmer Mark Spitz. In 2008, Phelps broke Spitz's record with eight gold medals in Beijing, and officially moved into his own category of elite performance. After those Games, he boldly stated that "records are always made to be broken no matter what they are … Anybody can do anything that they set their mind to."[1]

At age twenty-three, he had achieved all of the goals that he set for himself as a child. He had reached the pinnacle of sport, an achievement recognized by *Sports Illustrated* that named Phelps the "Sportsman of the Year." You might think that all of these accolades would be enough to make Phelps happy with a job well done, but instead he was left feeling empty and without purpose. The driving force that had guided his every move was no longer there, and his life began to veer off track as he turned to external sources of chemical relief to fill this new void. In 2009, he received a three-month suspension after a picture of him smoking weed went viral. As he began training for his next Olympics, he lost all motivation and his coach had to all but physically drag him to the pool each day. By the time the 2012 London Games came around, he had gotten to the point where he couldn't even look at a pool without feeling ill.

He got through London with four gold medals—again a better performance than any other athlete, but well beneath the standard he had already set for himself. At the end of those Games he announced his retirement from the sport, telling the press, "I'm done. I'm finished.

I'm retired. I'm done. No more." Later, he would admit that "I just wanted to be done with swimming and didn't want anything to do with the sport anymore."[2]

The suffering that Phelps was experiencing only got worse after he walked away from the sport, with rock bottom coming in 2014 when he was arrested for his second DUI. The next day, he curled up in his room and cried, and for the first time thought about ending his life. A man without a goal, he felt no more purpose in living. In his attempt to become the greatest swimmer of all time, he had lost his sense of who he was as a *person*. "Eventually," he said, "there was one question that hit me like a ton of bricks: Who was I outside of the swimming pool?"[3]

Although he felt totally isolated in his depression, he later learned that he was far from alone. In his 2020 HBO documentary *The Weight of Gold*, Phelps claimed that "a good 80% [of Olympic athletes], maybe more, go through some type of post-Olympic depression." And these post-Olympic blues, it seems, all share the same thing in common—an overwhelming deflation that comes from feeling like the athletes' goals are all behind them.

Elite snowboarder Shaun White tells his own story in this documentary, admitting that "after every Olympics, win or lose, I felt a dramatic emptiness, just because your whole world is built around this one day … there's this incredible crash. Nothing really matters as much anymore." As the record-breaking speed skater Apolo Ohno put it, "It's gold and then … what?"

Fortunately, Phelps was able to survive his suicidal thoughts, but others have not been so fortunate. According to olympedia.org, 164 Olympians have committed suicide since the Games began in 1894, a number that has likely increased since this book has gone to print.[4] Olympic bobsledder and gold medalist Steve Holcomb described his own experience with depression, confessing that "once it kind of starts going it just puts you into a spiral and you just start getting deeper and deeper into it, and just end up doing crazy things." After his first attempted suicide, Holcomb warned that "this is like an epidemic … there's a lot of people out there who are suffering through this."[5] In 2017, Holcomb's teammate found his body in his room at the Team USA training facility, where he had been dead for over two days after taking his own life.

"We're lost," Phelps explains. "I think that's where a lot of it really comes from, is we're just so lost, because we just spent four years grinding for that one moment, and now we don't know what the hell to do."[6]

The same post-achievement crash plaguing Olympic athletes can be seen with other high performers, as well. Astronauts, for example, deal with a sense of deflation after they return from space. Buzz Aldrin, part of the first manned mission to the moon, opened up about his own bout of depression in his book *Magnificent Desolation: The Long Journey Back from the Moon*: "I wanted to resume my duties, but there were no duties to resume. There was no goal, no sense of calling, no project worth pouring myself into."[7]

You would think that achieving the highest levels of mastery would lead to a fulfilled, satisfied life. But in reality, the opposite effect tends to occur. The same drive toward goal achievement that provides top performers with so much purpose ends up working against them once they run out of goals to pursue.

It would make sense if this phenomenon were restricted to these elites, due to the extreme lifestyle required to reach the top of their craft. But the same thing can be seen with average people like you and me. Consider the dreaded "midlife crisis." When people start their career they often have lofty goals of what they want to accomplish, including material success and also simply the desire to create value in the world. But as they approach retirement in their later years, they realize that most of those goals are either behind them or are never going to happen, and that source of dopamine withers away. When that happens, none of the possessions or accolades that they have accumulated can fill the void they feel growing within them. Like the Olympians, they feel empty and without direction, and they try to fill that void with fancy things or extreme experiences.

Phelps can relate: "We are human beings just like everybody else … No matter how your career goes, or how long it lasts, there's one inevitable end we all have in common: retirement. It's not really natural … you've devoted your life to a pursuit of such a singular goal and then leave it all behind. There's that giant question: now what? And even bigger: who am I?"[8]

The truth is that we all experience our own version of this existential crisis on a regular basis, regardless of where we currently are in our journey. We run from one goal to another on the hamster wheel of a never-ending to-do list, and the gap between these goals leaves our brain scrambling to answer the questions *What's next?* and *What's it all for?* The lack of answers to these questions triggers a stress response that, over time, can build to overwhelming levels.

With so many distractions in our goal pursuits, it is no wonder that anxiety is the most common mental illness in the United States. It affects over forty million people every year, with nearly half that number developing into depression. A big part of this condition is feeling like our life goals lack a coherent order. We keep running along on the treadmill of life, checking items off our to-do list and pursuing one goal after another. We stay so busy that we think we surely must be doing the right thing—after all, look at how much we are getting done!

But after every task and every goal, there's a micro-crash as we are forced to stop, pivot, and choose a new one to pursue. When we set up our reward system around a particular goal, then we will only receive the happy, pleasurable, motivating energy of dopamine as long as that goal exists somewhere in the future. When it transitions to our past, the dopamine stops—and without a new goal to pursue, our evolutionary instinct for survival kicks in and fills the void with stress-inducing cortisol. The more we identify with goal achievement, the more we experience a post-achievement crash, and the higher the likelihood that we will develop anxiety and depression. No matter how fully we fill our days, there still seems to be something missing, and the same question haunts our souls: *what's next?*

The Ideal Goal

So what's the answer? Do we stop focusing on our goals altogether, to avoid the inevitable pain that we will face after they are achieved? That would create a whole different set of problems. Goals are fundamental to the human brain, the operating code on which it functions. They are how we identify as a person, both through the goals that we have achieved in our past as well as those that we still intend to pursue. Further, the pursuit of those goals is what triggers dopamine release in the first place. No, we don't need to give up on our goals, we need to make sure we don't run out of them.

The solution is to choose a "master goal" so far in the future, and so difficult to accomplish, that you will never actually achieve it. This is what I call the Ideal because it represents the best possible version of yourself, one that you can never fully realize but that you can spend your entire life pursuing. Essentially, the Ideal represents your personal purpose in life, your reason for living, the thing that guides all of your thoughts and actions.

If you thought about putting this book down at the first mention of "purpose," I hear you. This word has become diluted to the point where it has lost meaning, and we can no longer relate to it. Consider this apparent contradiction. If you Google the word purpose, over 9.6 *billion* results come up. On the other hand, the actual use of the word in the English language has steadily declined since the 1800s. We are all searching for our purpose, but we have given up talking about it because we haven't found the answers we have been looking for.

The problem with purpose is that it is abstract, which makes it difficult to define. What *exactly* is our individual purpose in life? I don't believe that any of us will ever fully know the answer to that question. And if we approach it with the intention of getting the "right answer," we will only be frustrated. But what if we don't need to have the right answer to still get the benefits that having a purpose can provide?

The modern English definition of purpose is "the reason for which something is done or created or for which something exists."[9] But the origin of the word, which comes from the Old French *purposer*, is "to propose." A more comprehensive way of thinking about purpose, then, is as a *proposed* reason for which something is done or created or for which something exists. In other words, it is a *suggested* master goal for your life. Not a perfect one, but a *useful* one.

We can spend our entire lives trying to come up with the actual reason for our existence—and still come up short. Or, we can spend an hour writing something down that we feel relates to what that answer might be, and then use what we came up with as a tool to guide us forward. That's the value of the Ideal.

By writing down this potential purpose for your life, you activate your brain's goal organization framework—essentially, your brain begins to develop a structure of goals to obtain the achievement of that purpose. From that point, you can then begin constructing a chaordic funnel of progressively more concrete and shorter-term goals that connect to that Ideal, and benefit from the positive energy of dopamine that this creates. The Ideal itself sits above the chaordic funnel, a constant source of potential energy that can be tapped into through the execution of aligned action. Rather than shutting down after you achieve a short-term goal, your reward system will continue functioning because it recognizes that it is just another step toward an even bigger goal in the future.

The Ideal Provides Perpetual Energy for the Chaordic Funnel of the I GOT This Framework

The ✦ Ideal

STRESS
STRESS
STRESS
STRESS
STRESS
STRESS
JOY
JOY
JOY
JOY
JOY
JOY

Identifying Your Ideal

The exercise that first helped me to identify my personal Ideal was found in Covey's *The 7 Habits of Highly Effective People*, where he provides a "funeral exercise" that helps to connect the reader to the version of themselves they wish to become before they die. While each of our life stories is different, they all have the same ending: death. Thinking about death can be scary, and even triggering, because it is inevitable yet outside our control. However, we do have the power to control the way we *think* about death and to use those thoughts as a way to more fully control the actions we take in the immediate future.

Psychologists refer to the act of thinking about death as *mortality salience*, and they have found that it can "motivate people to enhance their physical health and prioritize growth-oriented goals; live up to positive standards and beliefs; build supportive relationships and encourage the development of peaceful, charitable communities; and foster open-minded and growth-oriented behaviors."[10] That's because thinking about who we will be at the moment of death instinctively creates an image of the type of person we wish to *become* before we die. The way we become that person is through the goals we set to adapt and grow, and these goals lead to proactive actions that result in positive benefits.

In Covey's exercise, he asks his readers to meditate on their own funeral, thinking about who is there, which people speak, and what they say. Because this visualization occurs in a reverent place with those you care about most, the message of your life will likely not include the material rewards that you received but rather the things you did that had an impact on others. When you write those statements down, you now have a tangible place to start crafting your own personal mission that you can use to make those actions a reality.

The ancient Stoics had their own methods for leveraging the end of one's life as a guide for short-term goals. When Roman emperors returned to the capital after a victorious military campaign, they would be paraded in front of the cheering masses with a slave positioned directly behind them, whispering into their ear, "Memento mori," a Stoic mantra meaning *Remember you must die*. By thinking about the inevitability of their death, emperors were reminded that they were not gods, and also that they should not become satisfied with resting on their laurels.

This same mindset can be used regardless of one's station in life. Ultimately, it is not the contemplation of death that causes us to live well, but the action that this contemplation inspires. As the Stoic Emperor Marcus Aurelius reminded himself, "Let each thing you would do, say, or intend, be like that of a dying person."[11] Likewise, the Stoic philosopher Seneca wrote that we should "prepare our minds as if we'd come to the very end of life. Let us postpone nothing."[12]

Regardless of whether we write down a vision of our future life or even take time to think about it, it still exists within our subconscious and drives the way we think, act, and feel. Mihaly Csikszentmihalyi wrote that "each of us has a picture, however vague, of what we would like to accomplish before we die. How close we get to attaining this goal becomes the measure for the quality of our lives. If it remains beyond reach, we grow resentful or resigned; if it is at least in part achieved, we experience a sense of happiness and satisfaction."[13]

Even with short-term goals, our brains think about how to start by first considering an ideal result. Psychologists studying the art of setting goals have developed what they call control theory, which says that individuals take action by comparing a current state to an ideal future standard, as defined by a goal, and then adjust their behavior in a way that will move them closer to that standard. By writing down a version of this future standard that already exists in your mind, you are giving your brain a better opportunity to appreciate progress, and it rewards you accordingly.

Examples of the Ideal

This lesson is one that Phelps learned after his post-Olympic spiral, which he was able to stop in its tracks when he identified his own version of the Ideal. After contemplating suicide, he checked himself into a treatment center where he "spent the next 45 days building [himself] from the ground up." When he went into the center, he was a man without a goal. After he left, he had a new mission: *to help everyone he could who struggled with mental health issues.* This was not a goal that could ever be achieved, because there would always be more people who need help. But that's the whole point. Because he can pursue this new goal indefinitely, Phelps can begin reconstructing a new dopamine reward structure that can last a lifetime.

What happened after Phelps shifted his mindset is evidence that de-emphasizing big goals for a longer-term vision doesn't limit your ability to achieve—it enhances it. With a renewed focus on a greater purpose, he came out of retirement for the 2016 Rio Olympics and finished his career in style with five more gold medals. But then he kept on going. In 2017 he joined the board of the mental health company Medibio. Then, in 2020, he released his hugely successful documentary *The Weight of Gold* on HBO. He continues to achieve big goals—they just aren't all in the swimming pool.

If you look at any person who seems truly fulfilled in their life, you will likely be able to find a statement of purpose that guides their actions. Angela Duckworth's ultimate concern is "to use psychological science to help kids thrive,"[14] which is an effective Ideal goal because there will always be more kids who can use help. Marie Kondo's mission is to "spark joy" in people by helping them to declutter their lives—again, there will always be more people, and more clutter. Whatever your own version of the Ideal looks like, you can use it to guide you towards the goals that will make you more like the person you wish to become.

Find Your True North

The Ideal is like the North Star that sailors used as a guide when they were out at sea before compasses or satellite GPS technology were available. Were they trying to sail into space and touch the surface of the star? Of course not. They simply used it as a tool to serve their voyage's purpose of crossing the ocean. Likewise, the North Star of our Ideal serves as a direction, not a destination. We want to pursue it so that our dopamine reward system is activated. But we don't want to actually achieve it, or that same system would shut down.

What is the North Star guiding your life? It doesn't really matter what your version of the Ideal looks like, as long as you can write it down and return to it regularly, and you can connect it to more tangible life goals. The I GOT This framework provides a specific formula to help you come up with the Ideal, which you can access by visiting theideallife.com or by scanning the QR code at the end of Chapter 1. The process takes about an hour and ends with seven Vision Statements and corresponding Core Values, which are then connected into one Mission Statement and Mantra. But you don't have to follow our exercises to generate your own Ideal, and it doesn't have to match our formula—yours could be a written paragraph, or even just a sentence.

The Ideal of The I GOT This Framework

Mantra

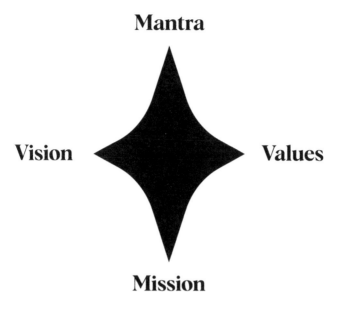

Vision   Values

Mission

My own personal Ideal includes a mantra to *Imitate Christ*, and a Mission Statement *to be a disciplined servant in body and mind in imitation of Christ, our King.* For me, this represents a goal of serving others, both directly through physical works and indirectly through the way I can share the lessons I've learned, and then I am able to connect that service back to my personal faith. I have also identified seven Core Values: Industry, Thrift, Love, Charity, Competition, Exploration, and Discipline—and each of those Core Values has its own Vision Statement that helps me to translate my Ideal into specific goals within each of my various life roles.

You can use the exercises at The Ideal Life to come up with an Ideal using the same model as mine, or you can come up with one on your own. I have also listed some prompts at the end of this chapter to help you get started.

Whatever your own Ideal looks like, or however you refer to it, just make sure it represents a long-term version for the type of person you wish to become. This will help you pursue short-term goals while still sustaining a joyful energy that comes from a lifetime of self-development. As the motivational speaker Jim Rohn put it, "Happiness is not contained in what you get. Happiness is contained in what you become."[16]

The Problem with Purpose

As powerful as purpose can be in setting up the framework of a joyful life, it has a problem. Precisely because it is so big and far in the future, it tends to be abstract. After all, what does it really mean to help kids thrive, to spark joy, or to imitate Christ? In order for effective goal pursuit to take place, there must be a specific outcome that we can fully focus on. The Ideal provides an ultimate concern that we can pursue indefinitely, but it is just the starting point of that pursuit.

In the next three steps of the I GOT This framework, you will learn how to identify a sequence of tangible, progressively shorter-term goals that help bring the vision of the Ideal into focus and create action out of its potential.

Ideal Reflection Questions

These reflection questions are designed to help you think about the lessons introduced in this chapter and begin brainstorming about how you could come up with your own personal Ideal. For a step-by-step guide of how to follow the specific steps of the I GOT This framework, scan the QR code in Chapter 1 or visit theideallife.com.

1. Think about how you would want people to talk about the way you lived at the end of your life. Write as much as you can think of in ten minutes, and then circle any themes you recognize.

2. Connect these themes together into your Ideal (one over-arching mission statement) that you can use as a guide for shorter-term goals. It can be one sentence or one page, as long as you connect with it and can turn it into action.

3. Identify a two- or three-word mantra that resonates with you and captures the message of your Ideal.

The ◆ Ideal — Step 1: Identify Your Master Goal

Stress

Dream Goal — Step 2: Visualize (But Don't Fantasize)

Horizon Goal — Step 3: Outline the Story of Your Life

Milestone Goal — Step 4: Find the Sweet Spot of Success

Objectives — Step 5: Control the Controllables

Tasks — Step 6: Make Happiness a Habit

Joy

This — Step 7: Deliberately Flow

CHAPTER 3

Step 2: Visualize (but Don't Fantasize)

Dream Goals

"Obstacles are stepping stones that guide us to our goals."
—"LIGHT," PHISH

The next three levels of the I GOT This framework's chaordic funnel—Steps 2 through 4 of the framework—are all part of the "Goals" element of the I GOT This framework. Even though every element of the framework is technically its own type of goal, these three steps—which include Dream Goals, Horizon Goals, and Milestone Goals—are given the designation of "Goal" because they represent the types of outcomes that we generally think of when we consider what we want to accomplish in our life.

As you will learn in the next three chapters, the uncontrollable nature of major goal achievement can make it addictive if it becomes our only focus. However, our goals play an important role in joyful living because they can translate the abstract Ideal into a specific path of pursuit, and they also provide a measurement of forward progress as they are accomplished. By better understanding how the brain uses its goals in the pursuit of the Ideal, you can harness their power without allowing them to control your life. This is easier said than done, however, and the journey toward the Ideal can be a precarious path. Before we dive into Dream Goals, then, I'll explain how the I GOT This framework is carefully crafted to help you master the art of goal setting.

The Art of Goal Setting

If you have ever read a book on goal setting, or participated in a goal-setting workshop at work or school, odds are that you have run into the SMART acronym—Specific, Measurable, Achievable, Relevant, and Time-Bound. It is by far the most widely used method for constructing an effective goal, and for good reason. The criteria captured by these five descriptors reflect the scientific findings published by Doctors Edwin Locke and Gary Latham in their 1990 work *A Theory of Goal Setting & Task Performance*. When goals have very specific outcomes and an objective way of determining success, Locke and Latham found, they have a much higher chance of being achieved.

However, in my experience I have found that not all types of goals need to meet these criteria, and in fact in many cases they should not. For one thing, the field of positive psychology and other disciplines have revealed many new insights into the science of goal setting since the 1990s, and those lessons allow for a more nuanced approach to the strategic pursuit of purpose.

Additionally, my coaching experience has taught me that setting a SMART goal from scratch tends to create a resistance in people that

STEP 2: VISUALIZE (BUT DON'T FANTASIZE)

ends up preventing them from taking action altogether. That's because the natural inclination of the human brain is to find the easiest way of doing things in order to conserve energy, and pursuing a truly SMART goal is difficult to do.

For example, a SMART goal might be "to lose 5 pounds by the end of 8 weeks by consuming no more than 1,800 calories per day." A typical first goal from a coaching client, however, sounds more like "to lose weight and feel better." The vagueness of this goal subconsciously allows the client to hide from the potential failure of their results. Rather than fight this resistance, the I GOT This framework embraces it through an incremental progression through each of the SMART elements as you move from the abstract Ideal down into the ordered structure of the Task.

The ART of the Goal

S M A **R** T	Ideal
S M A **R** T	Dream Goal
S M **A R** T	Horizon Goal
S M **A R T**	Milestone Goal
S M A R T	Objectives & Tasks

The Ideal, which was introduced in Chapter 2, is Relevant—meaning that it is connected to the subconscious vision that you have for your life—but it lacks Specificity, an effective method of Measurement, by definition is not Achievable, and as such has no clear Timeline of completion.

The Dream Goal, which will be the focus of this chapter, is a long-term goal for your life that is technically possible to achieve but not necessarily likely to happen. Because the Ideal helps craft Dream Goals, they are inherently Relevant to your personal purpose, and they also add in another element of the SMART criteria by being Specific. This allows them to move your Ideal down the chaordic funnel of an inner goal hierarchy.

For example, I have a Dream Goal of hiking the entire Appalachian Trail, which I know I could do but am uncertain that it will ever happen. However, I can use the specificity of this dream to direct shorter-term goals that will help me to become a healthier, more adventurous version of myself that is more closely aligned with my Ideal.

In each of the remaining chapters of this book I will begin by showing how each element of the I GOT This framework incorporates additional elements of the SMART acronym, and in doing so helps your goals to become more structured and ordered. Additionally, I will explain how each element captures the latest science of goal setting and well-being and incorporates those lessons into a consistent pursuit of the Ideal.

Now, let's get back to the framework itself and its second step of crafting a Dream Goal.

Positive Fantasization: The Pitfall of Dreaming

We all have something that we know deep down is what we *really* want to accomplish in life, and for me that dream has always been to be a writer. In the fourth grade, my teacher gave our class an assignment to write a short chapter based on the book *Ben and Me*, which tells the story of Benjamin Franklin through the eyes of a mouse that lives in his fur hat. I went home that night and didn't stop writing until my parents made me go to bed, and the next day I brought in four and a half chapters about an entirely new adventure that the mouse and Franklin had gotten themselves into—much more than what the actual assignment had called for. Recognizing my passion for the project, my teacher encouraged me to begin practicing my craft by setting up a private workshop for me. And what did I do with that support? Hardly anything.

Don't get me wrong, the desire to write stayed strong throughout my childhood and into adulthood. Nearly thirty years later, hardly a day has passed that I haven't thought about this dream. When I was stuck inside a cubicle for ten hours a day, I wondered how much more rewarding life would be if its days were spent at a writing table instead. As I waited in line at the DMV, I daydreamed about the stories I could develop if I started bringing around a little notebook to jot my ideas in. During vacations with the family, I thought about how cool it would be if I were skilled at describing scenes, so that I could journal about our trips and have a written memory book to enjoy with my wife and kids as we remembered our time together.

With all of that daydreaming, you would think that I would have about a dozen books published by now, right? You would be wrong. Up until I started working on this book in 2020, I spent hardly any time practicing the skills required to be a decent writer. I used my daydreams as an escape from the chaos of my life, rather than as a plan to take control of my future. I couldn't *actually* be a writer, I told myself. That was for people different from me, people who actually knew what they were doing. I needed to focus on getting good grades and then doing well at work, on being the type of person that my family expected me to be (which was another lie I told myself, because both of my parents, and then later my wife, have always actively encouraged me to write). I heard the voice inside me telling me to pursue my dream, and I told it to be quiet. Maybe next year.

Dr. Gabrielle Oettingen calls this type of unproductive dreaming *positive fantasizing*, and studies have shown that it actually saps you of energy rather than releasing more of it.[1] It's not that you don't actually want to make progress toward realizing the goal. In fact it's quite the opposite—you want it more than anything, which is why you spend all of your time thinking about it. Positive fantasization works against you because it doesn't do anything to bring you down the chaordic funnel from visualization into the action required to realize that vision. One study on this describes these dreams as depicting "an *idealized* version of the future that may include the attainment of desired future outcomes, as well as smooth, idealized processes of working toward these outcomes."[2] Essentially, the daydream is acting as the Ideal, but not providing a more specific plan of pursuit.

Positive fantasizing is a common problem, in part because it is fun to do. An entire industry has developed that caters to this indulgence, perhaps best embodied by the film titled *The Secret*. This Netflix documentary claims successful people have a secret that they want to keep from you, which is that you can manifest anything you want into reality *just by thinking about it*. In addition to achieving major life goals, they claim, you can also turn red lights green and create available spots at a full parking garage. They call this power *the law of attraction*, and profess that it is as consistent as gravity and physics.

The problem, though, is that it doesn't actually work. Visualization is important, but the only way to actually make things happen is by working at them. Sitting around thinking about where you want to go doesn't get you out the door. The real secret to realizing our dreams should be an obvious one: it takes a lot of hard work and discipline to achieve the goals we set for ourselves. And besides, the previous chapter explained why, from a happiness standpoint, you wouldn't want to get everything you wanted without work anyway. Dopamine is triggered by goal *pursuit*; if that pursuit never happens, then the dopamine will never come.

The Benefits of Visualization

One reason why fantasies don't manifest into reality is because they only include what you want to be there. Because we want our daydreams to be fun, they typically don't include all of the inevitable challenges that are likely to come up in real life. For example, it's really enjoyable for me to think about how nice it would be to wake up at 5:00 a.m. and make myself a pot of coffee, then sit outside on the porch as the sun rises and journal about a book outline I'm working on. What's *not* enjoyable is thinking about that routine getting interrupted by my thirteen-month-old son waking up at 5:05 a.m. and needing me to hold him until it's time to get the other three kids up for school—but that's exactly what ends up happening. My daydreams don't plan for that reality, and so dreams they remain. I still enjoy thinking about them, but as Dr. Oettingen warns, "indulging in visions of a positive future without figuring out how to get there … has short-term payoffs but long-term costs."[3]

Fortunately, there is a way to have your cake and eat it, too. Dr. Oettingen's studies show that positive visualization does, in fact, lead to a significantly higher likelihood of achieving your dreams, as long as you *do it the right way*.[4] Part of why movies like *The Secret* are so popular is because there are amazing stories out there of people who visualized their success so specifically that it seemed almost like magic when their dreams actually came true. Consider the story of Jim Carey, a one-time struggling actor whose career has developed into one of the most successful of all time.

Carey explained his early use of positive visualization on *The Oprah Winfrey Show*, telling Oprah, "I would visualize things coming to me that I wanted … I had nothing at that time, but it just made me feel better. At that time, all it really was for me was kind of making me feel better. I wrote myself a check for $10 million for acting services rendered, and I gave myself five years. I dated it Thanksgiving 1995, and I put it in my wallet and I kept it there. Then, just before Thanksgiving 1995, I found out I was going to make $10 million on *Dumb and Dumber*."[5]

This is where the proponents for the law of attraction stop the tape, saying, "See! All you have to do is write yourself a check and look at it every day, and the money will show up in your bank account!"

But if you keep watching for about fifteen more seconds, Carey delivers the punch line. As the crowd roars in applause for this amazing story, Oprah is almost drowned out when she follows with, "Visualization works, if you work hard!" Carey starts chuckling when he hears this, and the audience dies back down. "Well, yeah, that's the thing—you can't just visualize and then go eat a sandwich," he responds, laughing as if this were so obvious it didn't even need to be said. Our dreams help guide us forward, but only if we know the right way to pursue them.

Mental Contrasting

The solution to converting dreams into action, Dr. Oettingen says, is through a process that she calls *mental contrasting*.[13] There is now an abundance of scientific evidence showing that *positive* visualization provides the most benefit when it is immediately followed by *negative* visualization. You start by thinking about exactly how you want things to go, then immediately consider all of the challenges that are likely to disrupt that plan and how you might deal with them.

Dr. Oettingen has developed her own framework for helping people through this process, which she calls WOOP: Wish, Outcome, Obstacle, Plan.[14] First, you allow yourself the freedom to indulge in the daydream of what you Wish will come true in your life. Then, you add specificity to that wish by carefully detailing the actual Outcome you want to occur. After that you list out the Obstacles that you are likely to face, and then finally you make a Plan for how you will deal with those challenges.

After learning about the WOOP framework, I revised my fantasy of becoming a writer to a more specific Dream Goal. First, I thought about how my Wish to be a writer was connected to my overarching Ideal to *Imitate Christ*; by telling stories about the human condition, I could live into my Christian ideals of helping others and spreading love. Then, I made the Outcome more specific: rather than just wanting to be a writer, I set a more tangible dream of publishing a popular fantasy fiction series, like my favorite authors J.R.R. Tolkien, C.S. Lewis, and Robert Jordan. One of my biggest Obstacles was the lack of experience in creating published work, and so I made a Plan to begin by writing nonfiction, starting with this book.

Gabrielle Oettingen's WOOP Model for Mental Contrasting

Wish	Become a best-selling fiction writer
Outcome	Publish a popular fantasy fiction series
Obstacle	Lack of experience
Plan	Write a non fiction book

Now that I am getting into the final edits, I see my path toward my Dream Goal more clearly than ever. But it hasn't been without its challenges. In the three years it has taken me to complete this project, I have run into every roadblock I could have imagined, and then some. There have been multiple occasions when I have broken down in tears of frustration. I have felt like an amateur, a fraud, and a drain on other people's resources. But I knew these tough times would come, so I just kept on moving forward. In the end, the stress of this project helped fuel the energy required to complete it. Is the final outcome perfect? Of course not—no human product is. But it doesn't need to be perfect to serve the purpose of creating joy—it just needs to be one step closer to an even bigger goal still in the future.

The Greatest of All Times

Dreaming is an extremely helpful way to map out a path to the North Star of your Ideal, as long as those dreams have a way of coming out of the clouds and down to earth. When Michael Phelps achieved unprecedented heights through his sport, he told his fans to "Dream as big as you can dream, and anything is possible … Sometimes I have to pinch myself to make sure it is real."[15] Take one look at Phelps's muscular physique, though, and you will know that he put in the work to make his dream a reality.

One reason we love to watch athletes like Phelps is because we get to experience them living out the same dreams we had when we were children. Sports are also a classic example of a chaordic funnel, converting the passion for competition into an energy that transforms bodies and minds into an observable demonstration of mastery. The process that athletes undergo to achieve elite performance is no different from the one you and I can leverage in our own pursuit of joy, and many athletes are able to use their knowledge of that process to transcend their sport and make an impact in other life roles. Take Muhammad Ali for example, whose life reflects the lessons of this chapter and the power of positive visualization in the deliberate pursuit of an Ideal.

Born with the name Cassius Clay in 1942 segregationist Kentucky, Ali lacked the natural ability that defined most boxers of his generation. In fact, when he got his first shot at the title against Sonny Liston in 1964, the arena was half empty because no one thought that he had a chance of winning. As psychologist Carol Dweck explains,

> "Boxing experts relied on physical measurements, called 'tales of the tape,' to identify naturals. They included measurements of the fighter's fist, reach, chest expansion, and weight. Muhammad Ali failed these measurements. He was not a natural. He had great speed but he didn't have the physique of a great fighter, he didn't have the strength, and he didn't have the classical moves. In fact, he boxed all wrong."[16]

What he did have, Dweck would go on to explain, was a *growth mindset* that allowed him to grow into his potential. Part of that mindset included beginning with an Ideal that he knew he could pursue indefinitely, which wasn't fighting—it was to achieve complete freedom and independence from the stereotypes and social structures of his time.

"I had to prove you could be a new kind of Black man," he said. "I had to show that to the world." Boxing, he claimed, was just a means to that end: "I started boxing because I thought this was the fastest way for a Black person to make it in this country."[17]

He started with a dream. From the moment he put on his first pair of gloves at twelve years old he declared that he would be "the greatest of all time." Every night when he came home from the gym, he would tell his parents that he was going to become the champion of the world. He used this dream to fuel his ambitions, choosing to believe in a goal for himself that he knew most thought was unachievable.

Unlike me, who had a childhood dream and then spent most of my young life not doing anything with it, Muhammad Ali developed an incredible work ethic in the pursuit of his vision. He treated his body like the powerful machine he wanted it to become, avoiding alcohol and tobacco and even soda, which he thought was "as lethal as cigarettes." His biographer David Remnick was in awe of his dedication to discipline even in grade school, writing that "He woke between four and five in the morning, ran several miles, and then worked out at the gym in the afternoon, staying long past the hour when his peers had gone home for dinner," and that by the time he became a professional he had already become "one of the hardest-working athletes anyone had ever seen in Louisville."[18]

But even with his relentless focus on what he needed to do in the present, Ali still placed a huge priority on his visualizations for the future. Like Jim Carey writing himself a check, Ali carefully crafted a very specific outcome for his fights. When he was only fifteen years old, he announced that he was going to win the gold medal in the Rome Olympics—and he did. After his first fight as a professional, he exclaimed that he would become the heavyweight champion of the world—and he did. Early in his career, he made his first specific prediction in a fight, claiming that he would knock out Lamar Clark—a heavyweight with forty-five consecutive knockouts of his own—in the second round, and he did. As Remnick wrote, "he just kept predicting and winning, predicting and winning."[19]

Ali's ability to visualize the future was so uncanny that some might believe his results to be the magic of the law of attraction at work. But he didn't just think about what he wanted—he created a plan to turn that vision into a reality. You can see the extent of Ali's planning in the way that he explains his eighth-round prediction of his first Liston knockout:

> "You know, a fighter can condition his body to go hard certain rounds, then to coast certain rounds. Nobody can fight fifteen rounds. So I trained to fight the first two rounds, and to protect myself from getting hit by Liston.
>
> I knew that with the third, he'd start tiring, then he'd get worse every round. So I trained to coast the third, fourth and fifth rounds. I had two reasons for that. One was that I wanted to prove that I had the ability to stand up to Liston. The second was that I wanted him to wear himself out and get desperate. He would be throwing wild punches, and missing. If I just did that as long as he lasted on his feet, I couldn't miss winning the fight on points.
>
> And so I conditioned myself to fight full-steam from the sixth through the ninth round, if it lasted that long. I never did think it would go past nine rounds. That's why I announced

I'd take him in eight. I figured I'd be in command by the sixth. I'd be careful—not get hit—and I'd cut him up and shake him up until he would be like a bull, just blind, and missing punches until he was nearly crazy.

And I planned that sometime in the eighth, when he had thrown some punch and left himself just right, I'd be all set, and I'd drop him. Listen here, man, I knew I was going to upset the world!"[20]

To the public, it seemed like Ali had a crystal ball in his corner. But was this the law of attraction working its magic, or was it the inevitable result of careful planning in the relentless pursuit of a dream? I think the latter. And if you want to know the real reason why he was able to achieve that dream, I believe you need to look past it to his Ideal. If all Ali cared about was becoming the best boxer in the world, he would have experienced a Phelps-like crash after beating Sonny Liston to become the heavyweight champion of the world, at the young age of twenty-two. But he cared about more than that—he cared about achieving the type of independence that would advance the entire Black community.

Just three years after that first title fight, he had an opportunity to pursue this Ideal in a way that he could never have achieved in boxing. In 1967 he was drafted by the US Army to fight in the Vietnam War, and he refused. When the world's greatest fighter said he was choosing not to fight, the world was eager to hear his reason why.

When he famously stated that his reason was because "I ain't got no quarrel with them Viet Cong," he was establishing his independence from what he considered to be unethical mandates of the US government. By doing so, he created a model for other Black Americans to establish the same separation from racist legislation and helped set the stage for Martin Luther King, Jr. to pursue his own dream for racial equality.

The Path of Pursuit

Muhammad Ali understood the impact that vision has on the ability to be successful in life. "Champions aren't made in gyms," he said. "Champions are made from something they have deep inside of them—a desire, a dream, a vision." But his story also shows the importance of short-term progress on the path toward the Ideal. Not all of us will actually achieve the Dream Goals we establish for our lives—but that's OK, because the primary function of our dreams is to serve as a direction to guide the goals that we believe we can *actually* accomplish. The remaining steps of the I GOT This framework are all achievable, because the brain eventually needs to recognize how our visions will come into focus. Where the Dream goal represents a Wish in Oettingen's WOOP model of mental contrasting, our Horizon and Milestone Goals represent the Outcomes that we know we can achieve, and the Objectives and Tasks provide the Plan to overcome the Obstacles in the path to success. In the next chapter, we will look at how planning Horizon Goals can help create an outline of that success story, and set the stage for success.

Dream Goal Reflection Questions

These reflection questions are designed to help you think about the lessons introduced in this chapter and begin brainstorming about how you could come up with your own personal Dream Goals. For a step-by-step guide of how to follow the specific steps of the I GOT This framework, scan the QR code at the end of Chapter 1 or visit theideallife.com.

1. Write down a "bucket list" of major goals that you would like to accomplish in your lifetime. Have fun with it—there is nothing too big for this list!

2. Choose one of these dreams and create a vision board made up of pictures that help visualize turning that dream into a reality. You can draw these images yourself or print them from the internet.

3. Now, mentally contrast that positive visualization by journaling about all of the challenges currently holding you back from pursuing this dream. Think about a plan for overcoming one of these challenges.

The ✦ Ideal ········· Step 1: Identify Your Master Goal

Stress

Dream Goal ········· Step 2: Visualize (But Don't Fantasize)

Horizon Goal ——— Step 3: Outline the Story of Your Life

Milestone Goal ········· Step 4: Find the Sweet Spot of Success

Objectives ········· Step 5: Control the Controllables

Tasks ········· Step 6: Make Happiness a Habit

Joy

This ········· Step 7: Deliberately Flow

CHAPTER 4

Step 3: Outline the Story of Your Life

Horizon Goals

"Misty ships on the horizon line
and the golden dome is waking."

—"BENEATH A SEA OF STARS," PHISH
(originally performed by Ghosts of the Forest)

The third step in the I GOT This framework is to map out a set of medium-term outcomes that establish a path forward toward the long-term destination of a corresponding dream. These are called Horizon Goals in the I GOT This framework, and they add a level of Achievability to the Dream Goal because you are confident that you will accomplish them (you just don't know when). They are Specific, Achievable, and Relevant to one of your Dream Goals, but you do not need to consistently measure your progress or commit to a definitive date.

 Horizon Goal

Specific, Achievable, and Relevant

The Ideal sets the direction, Dream Goals create a destination, and Horizon Goals map out the plan to get there. Horizon Goals play an important role in advancing the Ideal down the chaordic funnel, helping to unlock the chemical reactions that lead to a joyful life. They help to bring the Dream Goal closer into focus by creating an actual outcome that we expect to achieve, while also leaving space to plan for the future without the restriction of committing to actual time frames. In this chapter we will look at the role that Horizon Goals play in outlining the story of your life and providing you with a path towards your Ideal.

The Role of the Horizon

In the physical world, the horizon has quite literally influenced the way our inner reward systems evolved. While hunting, our early ancestors would scan the horizon for signs of life, and during this process the ability to calm down and focus on the task at hand was paramount to success. Over time, our inner reward systems evolved so that looking toward the horizon triggered internal mechanisms that lowered our internal stress levels, which made our ancestors even more efficient at hunting. Although most of us don't rely on a daily hunt for our food, we still benefit from softening our focus and looking into the distance. Think about the last time you gazed out at the ocean or at an open plain. There is something about that view that calms you down, and this is because of an ancient physical process.

Goals Provide the Path to the Ideal

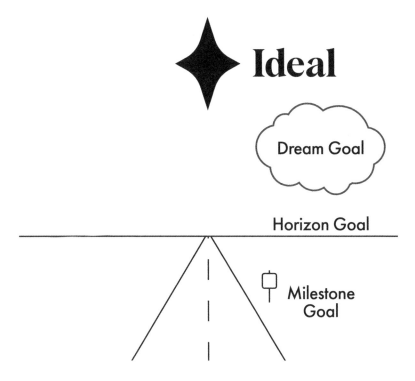

Similarly, Horizon Goals provide just enough detail to provide direction, but are still far enough away where we can't focus on the details. This allows us to benefit from the energy of the goal pursuit without feeling the stress of confronting our failures. An example of a Horizon Goal might be to run a half-marathon when you are still just training for a 5K, to get a promotion even though you just got hired, or to lose fifteen pounds over a year from now right as you are starting a new diet.

This runs counter to the way most of us try to set goals. Rather than look out toward the horizon, we tend to set our sights immediately in front of us. When we are singularly focused on our short-term goals, we want to achieve them NOW. Why think about losing fifteen pounds in a year when we want to lose five pounds by the end of this month?

We immediately jump into a short-term focus, whether it's getting an A on an upcoming term project, winning the next soccer game, or any other reward in one of our various life roles. These still might be fine goals to pursue, but if they are your singular focus then they will work against you. For one thing, if you aren't successful at them then you will be more stressed than when you started; and if you do achieve the goal, then you will experience the dreaded dopamine gap of *what's next?*

On the other hand, if your short-term goals are connected to a longer-term Horizon Goal, then both successes and failures can be connected to the same path forward. Let's say you only lost two pounds this month, when you wanted to lose five—you may have come up short in the near term, but you are still on track for the longer-term goal. This approach really helped me when I was training for my first marathon. If I missed a workout or got sick, I didn't freak out about missing that week's goals because I knew I still had many months before my race. This allowed me to stay consistent and not give up. By creating your own sequence of Horizon Goals, you can maintain the same type of distant vision that will allow you to stay the course rather than get sidetracked by near-sighted distractions.

Mapping the Horizon

I have found that I am best able to identify a Horizon Goal by starting with one particular Dream Goal and then working my way backward to establish its potential path of achievement. At each step I ask myself, *What would I need to have done first to achieve this goal?,* until eventually I get to something that meets the criteria for a Horizon Goal (in other words, I am confident I could eventually achieve it).

For example, one of my Dream Goals is to compete in the Ironman Triathlon World Championship in Kona, Hawaii. In order to do this,

I would first need to win a qualification event, which I'm not sure if I would ever be able to do. In order to do that, I would need to be able to win a half-Ironman-distance race, and before I could do that I would need to be able to finish a race in less than five hours. Finally, this would require running the half-marathon portion of the race in less than an hour and forty-five minutes. My best half-marathon time to date is just a little longer than that, so I know if I continue to train then I could get to that point.

Running a half-marathon in an hour and forty-five minutes has become my Horizon Goal, and now I also have a sequence of progressively less achievable future goals beyond the horizon that help connect it to my Dream Goal of going to the Kona World Championships. As I trace that path even farther into the future, I can see the outline of the story of how I will pursue my Ideal. By pushing my body and maintaining the level of health that would allow me to pursue these goals, I will be becoming a better version of myself, one that will be able to live longer and be more present in the lives of my children and future grandchildren and great-grandchildren. It's important to always keep in mind how the pursuit of our goals is helping us to develop into this ideal future version of ourselves, because this allows for a sustainable source of dopamine and helps to avoid a catastrophic cortisol crash.

A helpful tool in connecting this story together is through what I call a story "STIC" (pronounced like "stick"), which like a walking stick helps to guide you from one waypoint to another along your journey. This STIC stands for "*So That I Can …* " Watch how I use it to connect my future goals together:

Horizon Goals Bring Your Dream Goals Down to Earth

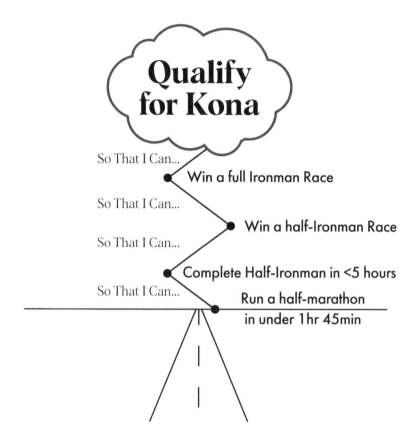

Starting from the Horizon Goal and working my way up, I can see a progressive path to achieving my Dream Goal. First, I will run a half-marathon in an hour and forty-five minutes, *So That I Can* complete a half-Ironman triathlon in less than five hours, *So That I Can* win a half-Ironman event, *So That I Can* win a full Ironman, *So That I Can* qualify for the Kona World Championships. Most importantly, the STIC can go even further in connecting that Dream Goal to the sustainable dopamine source of my Ideal. Why do I want to qualify for the Kona World Championships? *So That I Can* remain physically fit and mentally present in the lives of my children, grand-children, and great-grandchildren.

You can follow this exercise to map out a Horizon path for any of your Dream Goals. For example, maybe you have a dream of running a foundation that provides clean drinking water to a million people in developing nations. Here's a potential path that tells that story: *First, I will volunteer forty hours this year with a handful of different charities,* So That I Can *choose an organization to begin working with full time,* So That I Can *learn enough to start my own foundation,* So That I Can *grow that foundation into my Dream Goal of providing clean drinking water to a million people in third world countries.*

You can also use Horizon Goals to deal with challenges that have been forced upon you. For example, consider someone who has recently suffered a stroke and has lost the ability to communicate effectively. Their dream could be to be able to speak coherently for an entire conversation with their children.

They might write the following: *First, I will relearn how to articulate words,* So That I Can *articulate an entire coherent sentence,* So That I Can *speak for at least five minutes,* So That I Can *maintain an entire conversation with my children.* At the moment having a conversation might seem like an impossibility, too far over the horizon to seem reachable. But practicing a single word provides a challenging yet achievable step, and might eventually lead them to achieving their dreams. And even if it doesn't, they will have unlocked the joy of moving forward toward a better version of themselves, and that joy will help combat the anxieties of their diagnosis.

Outlining the Story of Your Life

Pursuing a goal without connecting it to a future one is like a writer completing a chapter without knowing what the rest of the book will be about. In the moment it might feel like the story is in a good place, but they are likely about to hit a writer's block because they don't know where the next chapter is going.

Early in the process of writing this book I learned the importance—and the joy—of creating an outline. While writing the first draft of the manuscript, I would spend about two weeks outlining each chapter before I even began writing. Two weeks! Every day I would go out onto the porch and write down topic ideas onto dozens of Post-it notes and then stick them onto the floor so that I could stand and look at them from a bird's-eye view. When I saw patterns connect I would move the notes around, until eventually they all flowed from one to the next in a coherent sequence.

As that last Post-it note fell into place, I would pump my fist and yell as if I had finished the book itself, because in a way, I had. Once I knew the major points I wanted to make, filling in the gaps became almost automatic. After the outline was complete, I would then sit down and hammer out the actual chapter in just a couple of days. The preliminary planning took time, but in the end it was the most efficient way to accomplish my goal.

The same thing happens when outlining the story of your life. A lot of planning goes into identifying the Ideal and then aligning the right Dream, Horizon, and Milestone Goals that map out a path to that purpose. But when your brain can easily recognize that your actions in the present moment are connected to a string of future goals, that planning pays off with the release of the motivating DOSE chemicals of your inner reward system. As you pursue these goals, dopamine is released that gives you energy and motivates you—and as you will learn in the coming chapters, oxytocin, serotonin, and endorphins are not far behind.

When outlining the story of your life, you can begin by defining your life roles and then establishing a clear path of goals within each one. Based on my research into the psychological study of human motivation, I have identified seven universal life roles—based on four fundamental human needs—that you can use to categorize how you will pursue your Ideal.

The Four Human Needs and the Seven Roles That Fulfill Them

In the first session of my Harvard course titled *Leading with Authenticity and Purpose,* our professor Dr. Ayse Yemiscigil asked us one simple question: "Who are you?" Our responses were all quite varied, but they had a common theme: "I'm an investment banker," someone started. "I'm a psychology major," another said. "I'm a soccer coach." "I'm a doctor." "I'm a mom." One after another, each student answered the question by defining their major life roles. This is how we process our self-identity.

If you are anything like me, you play many roles in your own life. I'm a husband, a father, a son, a brother, and a friend. I'm a CEO, an author, a board member, and a philanthropist. I'm an avid reader, a Phish fan, a Harvard graduate, and an Ironman triathlete. Above all, I'm a Christian. Depending on who I am meeting and in what context, I can choose from any of these roles as a way of introducing to someone *Who I Am.* Collectively, these roles also make up the perception that I have of my actual self, and the goals that I set within those roles paint the path toward my ideal self.

Our roles are critically important to our psyche because they are how the brain recognizes that we are fulfilling our fundamental needs. Every human has four basic needs, which I categorize as the "Four Cs": the need for Control, the need for Connection, the need for Competence, and the need for Clarity. Each one of these is directly tied to our overarching evolutionary need to survive and thrive. By breaking each of those needs into the roles that serve to fill them, we can identify a more intentional method of goal setting that focuses on what we need most in any season of life.

The Four Cs of Human Needs

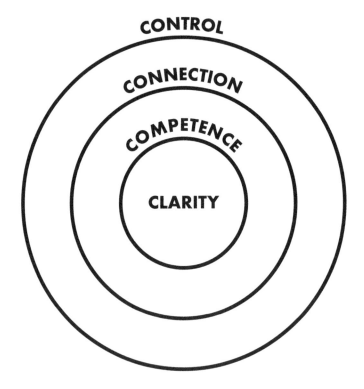

The Seven Roles That Fulfill Our Needs

WORK AND WEALTH: THE ROLES FOR CONTROL

Our need for control is directly tied to what psychologist Abraham Maslow referred to as our "basic safety needs." When our early ancestors were first emerging from their caves, they found safety in the secure dwellings and weapons that protected them from external threats. In today's society, we secure our shelter and security through the means of our personal savings, which we use to pay our rent and contribute taxes for the protection of the police and military. Our modern need for control, then, is primarily satisfied through the acquisition and development of personal savings.

You have probably heard the saying, "Money doesn't buy happiness." Unfortunately, that's not entirely true. Psychologists have found that having more money actually does lead to an increase in well-being, *up to the point that basic needs like food, shelter, and security have been met.* When the first studies came out in 2010 the average amount required to achieve this level of security in American households was around $75,000 per year—which would be somewhat higher now due to inflation—but the number itself is not as relevant as the point that it represents: if we can't control our basic needs, this leads to excessive levels of stress.

If you want to increase your savings, the first step is finding ways to earn more money. Then, you can focus on limiting your spending so your bank account eventually grows. We can identify two role categories related to our need for control, then: work and wealth.

Our work roles are often those that we identify with most closely. Think again about how you might answer that question: *Who are you?* For most of my career, my answer was "I work in logistics." Today, I might answer with, "I'm the founder and CEO of a growth mindset company." In the future, I hope to answer with, "I'm a successful fantasy fiction writer."

Whatever the unique role is that I identify with in that moment, the underlying need remains the same: in order to control the security of myself and my family, I need to work and create value in the world. You might work at a role that creates value but doesn't directly generate income, such as a full time parent or a nonprofit volunteer. These would also fit under this category.

The wealth roles that fulfill our need for control are not always as self-evident. After all, you don't hear many people say "I'm a checkbook balancer," or "I'm a family budget preparer." But in reality, this role category is critical and one that cannot be ignored in the pursuit of an Ideal Life. It doesn't matter how much we make if we are spending it faster than it is coming in. When we fail to look at our finances as a key focus of self-improvement, we do so at the risk of deteriorating our savings and exposing ourselves to threats against our personal security.

Ultimately, how we think about money plays a huge role in how we think about the world and our place in it. In one study, children from poor and wealthy families were each presented with objects that had the size and feel of coins such as dimes and quarters. Remarkably, the children from the poorer families subjectively perceived the size of those objects to be significantly larger than they seemed to the well-off children! Because their basic security needs had yet to be met, their subconscious placed a greater amount of attention and emphasis on money-related images that would help achieve goals related to increasing that psychological need.[1]

Similarly, if we don't have a clear plan of how we are managing our finances, then the anxiety of not feeling in control will dominate our subconscious and affect the way we look at all of our other goals.

FAMILY AND COMMUNITY: THE ROLES FOR CONNECTION

One of the best ways to satisfy our need for survival is to develop connections with other people, both directly and indirectly. From an evolutionary perspective, being part of a tribe reduces our chances of being exposed to an external threat because we are protected by those around us.

In order to encourage us to maintain our position within the group, the human brain motivates us to pursue two apparently conflicting goals: fitting into a group while simultaneously differentiating ourselves from that group. The second of these is important because if our early ancestors weren't creating unique value for their tribe, then they might have been seen as a drain on its resources and expelled from the group. When we feel good about ourselves after scoring a goal for our team, getting a promotion at our company, or even feeling appreciated by our family, that comes from our innate desire to stand out among those we want to fit in with.

The roles that fulfill our need for connection, then, can be divided to account for the goals related to both fitting in and standing out. I call the "fitting in" roles our *family roles* because they are best satisfied within our most direct relationships. Achieving goals within these family roles results in the release of oxytocin, which makes us feel loved and connected to others. Oxytocin generally requires close physical proximity in order to be released, such as direct eye contact, handshakes, and hugs, which is why these roles typically involve those closest to us. In humans, low levels of oxytocin have been directly associated with autism spectrum disorder, a condition that severely limits the ability to "understand or engage in social situations despite preserved intellectual abilities."[2] As a key component of social bonding, oxytocin reinforces our evolutionary need to be a "part of the tribe."

A great thing about our closest relationships is that they can remain strong even during long stretches of physical separation. Chelsea and I are both from Richmond, Virginia, and living in Charleston means that we only get to see our extended family a few times a year. But that distance doesn't diminish the love that we have for them, and vice versa. However, we can also take those relationships for granted. Just because they are strong doesn't mean we still don't need to work on them. The deliberate practice of our family roles is essential to maintaining the healthy relationships that fulfill our need for connection.

I call the roles that satisfy our need for standing out our *community roles* because we don't need to be physically present with someone to experience the pride of contributing to the group. These roles don't just involve community service; they can also include how we interact as neighbors, as citizens, and as members of the other various social groups we might choose to join.

Being social is a good thing—studies show that participating in groups and developing our identification with those groups lead to increased mood and longer life span.[3] These groups can be small, like a neighborhood book club, or big, like being an American. But either way, it's not enough to just *say* you belong to these communities—you need to *feel* like you belong by setting goals and working hard to contribute value to the rest of the group.

HEALTH AND WISDOM: THE ROLES FOR COMPETENCE

Psychologically, our brains are not satisfied with simply staying safe and bonding with others. Those things are important, but we also have a natural curiosity to explore what life could have in store for us personally, beyond our basic evolutionary goals. Maslow referred to this as the need for *self-actualization*,[4] which is our fundamental desire to make our current self align more closely with the ideal version of what we could become.

There are two main categories to self-actualization—physical and mental—which I categorize as our health roles and our wisdom roles. Our modern society often associates health with appearance, but usually what the internet tags as beauty is not actually healthy. Physical health requires pursuing goals that will then give your body the energy it needs to better achieve the goals you have established in your other life roles. That means consistent exercise, regular rest, a balanced diet, and effective stress management. All of these things have a dramatic impact on the release of inner chemicals that lead to a joyful life.

Just like health gets confused with appearance, wisdom is often mistaken for academic success, but you don't have to graduate from college to learn about the world. We all have a desire to learn more about something. I personally enjoy the structure of a school's classroom setting, and so I choose to pursue "intellectual" goals like my most recent master's degree from Harvard. On the other hand, I have a good friend who would be happy if he didn't have to answer another test question for the rest of his life, but he can tell me the stroke-to-bore ratio of a 6.7-liter Cummins truck engine. Whether it's psychology, diesel mechanics, or gardening, we all get joy from expanding our knowledge about something that interests us.

FAITH: THE ROLE FOR CLARITY

Just like every good story ties all of its loose ends together in its conclusion, our brain needs to understand how all of our life roles will ultimately connect within a bigger picture. We have a need for the clarity that everything we do is part of a bigger purpose, and our reward system is grounded in the faith that this purpose is being fulfilled.

The word faith is often associated with religion, but it is broader than that. The dictionary definition of faith is "complete trust or confidence in someone or something."[5] Faith is *what we* believe in; religion is one way we can choose to *express* that belief. You may identify as a Christian, a Jew, a Muslim, an atheist (having faith in the belief that there is no God), or any number of other belief structures. At our core, we all believe in something, whether we choose to acknowledge it or not.

When we experience our faith in action, we enter into a state of joyful awe that Maslow called *transcendence*.[6] These moments don't have to occur inside a church, synagogue, or mosque—they are often triggered by a particularly beautiful sunset or by the sound of a child's laughter. Amazingly, fMRI scans reveal that the same brain regions that light up during a religious experience are also active when we observe an awe-inspiring scene in nature.[7] Our brains enjoy feeling like we are a part of something bigger than ourselves, and they reward us for deliberately practicing the roles that allow for those experiences.

Writing the Next Chapter

Once you have outlined the major roles that you play in your life, you are ready to start the actual process of writing your story by selecting a Horizon Goal to pursue within one of those roles. But which one to work on first? To answer that question, the I GOT This framework uses a concept called the Pareto Principle.

The Pareto Principle, also called the Law of the Vital Few or the 80/20 Rule, is based on a finding made by the nineteenth-century Italian economist Vilfredo Pareto, who observed that roughly 20 percent of the population held around 80 percent of the country's wealth. Since then, a similar pattern has been seen in a variety of other contexts.[8] For example, roughly 20 percent of criminals commit 80 percent of all crimes, 20 percent of drivers cause 80 percent of all traffic accidents, and 20 percent of employees are responsible for 80 percent of their company's results. This phenomenon led the quality guru Dr. Joseph Juran to develop his own theory in the 1950s that said the majority of any system's results can be most directly influenced by focusing on just a "vital few" of its inputs.

When you look at the categories of your life, you can identify which "vital few" could have the biggest impact on your overall well-being. You may be naturally drawn to focus on the areas where you are already spending the most time (which is often the work roles for many people), but you can usually create a bigger effect by focusing on a role that you have been neglecting.

For example, if you want to improve your health but haven't worked on your closest relationships recently, you might be surprised by the energy that could be unlocked by deliberately practicing your family roles. This energy will then spill over into the other areas of your life, and you just might find that your health begins improving without even having to push yourself. As the saying goes, "A rising tide lifts all ships."

Once you have chosen the next life role to work on, you can use the Pareto Principle to select one Dream Goal within that role, and one Horizon Goal that would lead to that dream. Is this the only path toward the pursuit of your Ideal? No. But it is *a* path that you can be confident will guide your next steps forward in the right direction—and that's all your brain needs to trigger the release of joy that you are really looking for.

As tempting as it can be to consider all the different ways of pursuing the various goals in our life, the truth is that we can only experience the joy of thinking about those pursuits within the present moment, and we can only focus on one thing at a time. It is much better to stick with one goal, then, and one path of achieving that goal, to maximize the chemical sensations of motivation and satisfaction that come from its pursuit.

When we make progress toward our Horizon Goals, they eventually transition into the next goal we want to actually pursue. This is just like what happens when we are driving toward the real horizon. As we move forward, the objects that were once in the distance have now moved into the foreground, even though the horizon line remains fixed in the windshield. In the I GOT This framework, I refer to this transition as the shift from Horizon Goals to Milestone Goals, which will be covered in the next chapter.

When I first began this book three years ago, finishing it was a Horizon Goal for me. I was confident that I would get it done, but the monumental scope of the project was too much to pursue all at once. As I am writing this, the book is almost complete, and its publication has now become a Milestone Goal. I know that I am making progress toward my Ideal, and this progress has unlocked the joy of knowing I am on the right path. By answering the reflection questions below, you can begin mapping the horizon of your own journey.

Horizon Goal Reflection Questions

These reflection questions are designed to help you think about the lessons introduced in this chapter and begin brainstorming about how you could come up with your own personal Horizon Goals. For a step-by-step guide of how to follow the specific steps of the I GOT This framework, scan the QR code at the end of Chapter 1 or visit theideallife.com.

1. Using the seven categories of life roles introduced in this chapter, identify at least one specific role that you play within each category. If you can think of more than one, list all that come to mind.

2. Select the role that you feel you have focused on the least over the past three months. Using the "bucket list" that you came up with in Step 2, choose one Dream Goal that relates to this life role.

3. Using that Dream Goal, write down a list of three to four steps that would need to occur before that dream could become a reality.

The ◆ Ideal — Step 1: Identify Your Master Goal

Stress

Dream Goal — Step 2: Visualize (But Don't Fantasize)

Horizon Goal — Step 3: Outline the Story of Your Life

Milestone Goal — Step 4: Find the Sweet Spot of Success

Objectives — Step 5: Control the Controllables

Tasks — Step 6: Make Happiness a Habit

Joy

This — Step 7: Deliberately Flow

CHAPTER 5

Step 4: Find the Sweet Spot of Success

Milestone Goals

"You're on the highway now with higher hopes."

—"BLAZE ON," PHISH

Accomplishing goals feels good, but that feeling is dangerous when you make it your sole focus. In this chapter I will talk about the process of actually achieving the goals you set in your life, and how that forward movement can either bring you closer to your Ideal or lead you farther off the path. It all depends on finding the sweet spot of success.

If you picked up this book because you wanted to learn a better way to pursue the goals that are really important to you *right now*, then this is the chapter for you. The first three steps of the I GOT This framework have all been planning for the distant future—the Ideal, which represents a goal so far in the future that you'll never actually reach it; the Dream Goal, which is more tangible than the Ideal but not certain to be achieved; and the Horizon Goal, which you are confident you can accomplish but not in the immediate future. Now it is time to use that Horizon to set a Milestone Goal that you can begin working toward immediately.

 Milestone Goal

Specific, Achievable, Relevant, and Time-Bound

The Milestone Goal represents the successful outcome that you can achieve *right now*. It's the weight loss, or the work promotion, or the relationship healing that you believe is the next best step in the pursuit of the person that you wish to become. Just like mile markers along the side of the highway guide you forward toward the distant horizon, Milestone Goals inform your brain that you are making progress along the path toward your Ideal, and it is this forward movement that triggers the release of your inner reward system.

This chapter will help you understand the importance of goal achievement along the path toward your Ideal. But hopefully by now you have realized that the I GOT This framework is not just about goal success—it is primarily about the process of becoming a better version of yourself. However, accomplishing goals is a critical part of that journey. If you have taken the time to properly align your next major goal with longer-term stepping stones that lead to a personal vision of a fulfilled life, then you will be rewarded with the joy of feeling you are on the right path.

One paradox of this framework, however, is that when you de-emphasize your short-term results in exchange for a long-term vision, you will tend to have more immediate success anyway. After decades of focusing only on what was next in my life, I finally learned that lesson during my personal journey from being obese and sedentary to losing eighty pounds and completing a full Ironman Triathlon.

Becoming an Ironman

The year that I spent in a wheelchair marked a transition in my life in which I went from identifying as an active kid to someone who I believed could never be athletic again. I had played soccer since I was five years old, and had always prided myself on being the "fast kid" who could run up and down the field without getting tired. The ski accident happened shortly before I hit puberty, which meant that I ended up spending a lot of time sitting down doing nothing during a period when my body was trying to grow, change, and mature. So, rather than learn athletic skills and gain the experience of being on sports teams, I became awkward and spent a lot of time alone. Instead of growing stronger, like most of the other kids in my school, I started gaining unhealthy weight as I turned to junk food that I had no way of burning off.

By the time my leg healed, I had developed bad coping habits that stuck with me throughout high school and into college. To deal with the stress caused by my anxieties and poor lifestyle, I compounded the problem by turning to alcohol, cigarettes, and more junk food. In hindsight I now realize that I was self-medicating with quick hits of dopamine and serotonin that made me feel better temporarily, only to leave me with a chemical void that I became addicted to filling with progressively unhealthier options. Year after year I would try to break this cycle by attempting to diet or starting a new workout routine, but I could never seem to stick with any healthy plan for longer than a couple of weeks. Every time I slipped up, I would feel like a failure and fall even further off the wagon.

By 2016, I weighed over 235 pounds with hardly any muscle, and at age twenty-eight, my health was quickly deteriorating. I knew something had to give when I threw my back out while leaning over to change my daughter's diaper. *How could I teach my children how to be healthy*, I thought, *if I can't even take care of myself?* Up until that point, I had been using short-term goals as the direction for my attempts to diet or exercise. If I could just lose fifteen pounds, I would think, *then* I would be happy.

But then I had an epiphany. By that point, I had already begun developing the I GOT This framework and was applying it to my career with incredible results, and I wondered what would happen if I applied this long-term approach to my health. And so, as an experiment to see if the framework would apply to my other life roles, I decided to give it a try.

First, I connected my physical health to the long-term vision of my Ideal Life. I imagined myself at a hundred years old, a proud father, a grandfather, and a great-grandfather surrounded by the love of my family. In this vision, I was still mentally sharp and physically active—in fact, I could get down on my knees and play with the youngest of my great-grandchildren and get back up without help. I saw myself traveling with my family and being able to do all the things that the children wanted to do without holding anyone back.

With that Ideal in mind, I began researching athletic activities that were popular for older people, and during my search I stumbled across the sport of triathlon. I was immediately captivated. I learned that triathlon races, which include swimming, biking, and running, are structured around age groups, which means that individual participants compete against the other athletes that are their same age. In fact, an eighty-five-year-old had competed in and finished the sport's biggest event—the Ironman World Championship in Kona, Hawaii. Here was a sport where twenty-five-year-olds could compete against each other for an Olympic gold medal, and then go and race within a field that included athletes sixty years older than them!

I knew that this sport could provide a path to guide me forward for the long term. And so I set a Dream Goal of one day going to the Kona World Championships myself, even if that meant taking half a century to get there. With my Dream Goal in mind, I established a Horizon Goal of completing my first triathlon, and a Milestone Goal of finishing a five-kilometer (5K) run event in three months. Then, I got to work.

On the first day of my exercise journey, I told myself that I would run for thirty seconds. That's it. Even if I wanted to run longer, I would force myself to stop, turn around, and walk home. And that's exactly what I did. Not knowing "how" to run, I set off at a dead sprint for about five seconds, and in my poor physical shape my lungs immediately began to burn, and I slowed down. After about fifteen seconds, I could feel my shins and feet starting to hurt, and at the thirty-second mark I was glad to be able to stop. I knew I could have gone longer, but I also knew that the I GOT This framework requires baby steps to be successful. So I turned around and walked home, and that was it for the day.

Before developing the I GOT This framework, I would have started out that first day a lot differently. Instead of thirty seconds I would have tried to run thirty minutes, or at least have tried to finish a mile. What is thirty seconds going to do, I would have thought, especially if I'm trying to run a 5K race in only three months? I've got to get going if I'm going to achieve the goal!

The mindset of "do more, now" makes sense in a world without challenges and limitations, but that's not how life actually works. When we try to push ourselves too hard, too fast, we end up burning out, not achieving our goals and being more stressed than when we started. On the other hand, a "do a little more, and keep going" mindset allows for the consistency that leads to long-term success. It was difficult to see how a thirty-second run would get me ready for a five-kilometer race in three months, but I *could* visualize it leading to a healthier life fifty years from now—and that is where I was choosing to place my priorities.

A long-term focus like this actually ends up leading to short-term success because it keeps us from quitting. The reason for this involves basic math. Let's say you focus on a goal with a target completion date ten days from now. If you fail one day in executing the actions required to achieve that goal, that means you have missed out on 10 percent of the effort you had planned to put forth. That's a huge hurdle to overcome! On the other hand, if if that 10-day goal is just a step toward a much larger goal set fifty *years* in the future, then one day is now just 0.00005 percent of the total time you have remaining. Your short-term plans are identical in both situations, but your failures have now become 200,000 times less important. Rather than be derailed by those failures, you can learn from them.

That's what I was able to do in my health journey. The second day during my training, I set a goal to run thirty-three seconds—just 10 percent more than what I had done the day before. This was a nearly negligible step forward in the short term but one that was on the path toward my longer-term goals. As I walked back to the house, I remember the joy that came from knowing that I had made progress. Each day after that, I came back and ran just a tiny bit longer, and the incremental progress fueled the consistency that eventually led to a habit of being active. After a month I still hadn't completed a mile run, but my body was starting to hurt less, and I noticed that I began every day *wanting* to get out and run.

As I continued to make small increases in effort, those same percentages began to translate into much longer distances. By the end of the third month I was able to complete that 5K race (very slowly), and then I set another Milestone Goal of running a 10K. I achieved that one, too, and then ran a half-marathon later in the fall, and completed a full marathon in December. In one year thirty seconds had turned into four hours, but I never felt like I pushed myself too far, too fast.

The next year I began to incorporate a similarly "easy" approach to biking and swimming, and was able to finish my original Horizon Goal of completing a triathlon. Then, I set my sights on an even further horizon, and by the end of 2018 I completed a full Ironman Triathlon—a 2.4-mile swim, 112-mile bike, and 26.2-mile marathon, back-to-back-to-back! This race took me over fifteen hours to complete, much longer than the thirty-second run that got the journey started. In hindsight this seemed like a huge jump in only two years, but I could only have achieved it by setting my sights much farther into the future, to the life I wanted to live regardless of whether I achieved my shorter-term goals.

The Joy Is in the Journey

Now here is the most important part of this story: the feeling that I experienced as I crossed the finish line of that fifteen-hour Ironman felt *the same* as the joy that I experienced after the thirty-second run that started this triathlon journey. My long-term focus led to the achievement of progressively bigger short-term goals, but the *joy that I experienced from each goal remained the same*. This is because the amount of feel-good dopamine that was manufactured and released to reward me for the pursuit and accomplishment of each goal was essentially identical, because each one represented the next step forward in the pursuit of a larger goal.

This might seem crazy to you—how could a thirty-second run compare to a fifteen-hour endurance event? But it makes sense when you consider my ability *immediately preceding* both of these outcomes. In 2016, I was sedentary and obese and had not run for exercise in nearly a decade. For that version of myself, running thirty seconds was a big leap from anything I had done before. By 2018, however, I had gradually scaled up to where I was actually completing Ironman-distance workouts during my training sessions. When it came time to actually race, I was simply stringing those workouts together to complete an event that had become just a little bit outside of my comfort zone.

The takeaway here is that you shouldn't give too much mental real estate to the anticipation of some big future goal by making it the primary source of your future happiness. If you pursue that goal in the right way, then by the time it arrives it will no longer be a giant leap—it will just be the next step forward. It will feel good to accomplish that goal, but it will also feel good to reach all the little steps that led to that milestone.

Further, it is important to remember that the joy from our big goals won't last forever. The chemicals that are released are the same for each goal pursuit, and those chemicals always fade away. It is foolish to think that there is some magic goal achievement that will lead to lasting happiness; it is wiser to plan a path of goal pursuit that creates a sustainable source of joy and learn how to savor each of those moments along the way.

Savoring Success

There is an art to finding the right amount of focus to apply to short-term goals—not too much, not too little. Too little emphasis on goal achievements creates a deficiency in the chemicals that motivate us and bring us joy, while focusing on them too much leads to an addiction to those chemicals that can derail us from the path toward our Ideal.

First, let's look at why allowing yourself to appreciate the good outcomes in your life is important. In fact, appreciating the good feeling that comes from success is a key component of mental health. Psychologists refer to this as savoring, and it has been linked to a wide spectrum of positive outcomes. One scientific definition of savoring is "attending to, appreciating, and enhancing positive experiences that occur in one's life."[1] It's OK to feel good, and we shouldn't try to avoid opportunities to do so.

After I completed the Ironman event, I was blessed to be able to enjoy the accomplishment with my family. My wife was the only one who saw everything that it took to prepare for the race, and her embrace at the finish line helped affirm everything I had gone through to reach that point. Hearing my daughter tell me she was proud of me moved me to tears and helped me to connect the race with my Ideal that was still there driving me forward. Even my dad traveled to see me compete, and no matter how old I get, it always feels good to think that I've made my parents proud.

But after we drove back to Charleston and I hung my medal on the garage wall, I knew I had to turn my attention to deliberately improving my abilities in another life role so that I could maintain a balanced pursuit of the Ideal. This was difficult to do because I wanted to dive even deeper into the success that I had experienced in pushing my athletic boundaries. But I knew that if I didn't place the same type of focus on improving the roles in my faith, family, and finances, then that singular drive toward athletic achievement would actually lead me away from the person I wanted to become.

The Pitfall of Pleasure

As beneficial as it can be to savor the positive effects of goal achievement, placing too much priority on those chemical rewards can lead to addiction. The reason for this is that our major goals are usually uncontrollable. Getting a promotion depends on our boss to make that decision. Healing a relationship requires the other person to meet us halfway. And even completing a race depends on all of the other people to show up. I trained for nine months for the 2018 Ironman Florida event in Panama City only for it to be canceled when Hurricane Matthew wiped out the Florida panhandle. It was the last race of the season that I could participate in, and I knew I would have to pause my training because Caroline was about to be born. Luckily they made a last-minute decision to move the race to Haynes City, and I still achieved my goal of completing an Ironman-distance race—but only because of other people's hard work in making the event happen.

It is the uncontrollable nature of goals that make them so exciting when we achieve them. For example, think about the reaction that you see on an athlete's face after they score a goal or win a big competition. They jump up and down, pump their fist in the air, and hug their teammates. This type of reaction doesn't happen because they always knew what the end result was going to be. It happens because they knew they were able to influence a positive result that they did not actually control. But as exciting as it can be to not know if we will succeed or not, this critical component of goal setting also comes with a massive pitfall: addiction.

In the 1940s, the behavioral psychologist B.F. Skinner demonstrated the addictive nature of inconsistent, uncontrollable rewards. He began by using pigeons, and later replicated the same results in humans. Skinner created a contraption that he called an operant conditioning box, in which a pigeon was given food as a reward for pecking at a lever. Some pigeons received food every time they pecked at the lever, while other pigeons were only randomly rewarded. After a set period of time, both levers stopped providing anything at all.

The differences in how the pigeons behaved between these two types of reward schedules were striking. The consistently rewarded pigeons quickly learned how to get their prize, but after the food stopped coming it did not take them long to realize that they should stop hitting the lever. The pigeons receiving a reward they could not control, on the other hand, pecked longer at the lever after the food stopped coming. A LOT longer. In some cases, the pigeons pecked over *150,000 times* without a single reward! They were willing to waste an incredible amount of energy in the hopes that the next peck might give them the reward they had come to crave.[2]

Similar studies found the same pattern of behavior in humans.[3] If we experience a consistent reward, we appreciate it while it's there, but we are able to move on when it disappears. When those rewards are hit or miss, we quickly grow an addiction to waiting for their arrival. There is something about wanting things out of our control that makes us crave them to the point where we can't even control ourselves.

Big corporations paid attention to Skinner's studies and quickly used them to their advantage. For example, the slot machine is a direct result of his findings, a modern-day operant conditioning box for humans that keeps them sitting in a chair pulling a lever for hours, until they have lost all their money and have to go home.

Social media is another example. In today's society, the biggest manipulators of our internal reward systems are the social networks like Facebook and Instagram, who have used their own understanding of the human design to condition their users' behaviors. The intricacy of these algorithms was exposed in the Netflix documentary *The Social Dilemma*, in which ex-executives of the biggest social media networks explained exactly why they would never allow their own children to use the very system that they created.

By teaching us to associate virtual interactions with our deeply embedded needs for bonding and respect, social networks have established an intermittent reward system that keeps the public hooked on their services. When we get a friend request, we feel like we have successfully bonded. When our selfie gets a like, we feel like we have earned respect. As sophisticated as our brains are, they can't tell the difference between these virtual triggers and the physical ones that we evolved to pursue. By carefully crafting their algorithms to provide a random release of dopamine, oxytocin, and serotonin, social media networks wage a dirty war against the human psyche in exchange for their own reward of massive advertising revenue. While the social media giants make billions on advertising dollars, their users give away control over their personal happiness.

The Hedonic Treadmill

We don't need evil corporations to manipulate us—we do it to ourselves. When we focus primarily on the outcomes of our big, uncontrollable goals, a single-minded pursuit of their achievement can lead to a similar type of addictive behavior. Because the chemical rewards of goal achievement are outside of our control, this sets up a situation in which we become addicted to the pursuit of the pleasure that they provide.

This is what happens when we put too much focus on the feeling that comes along with buying fancy things with the money we get from doing better at work, or the perceived respect we get from an important sounding title. It might feel nice in the moment, but that feeling disappears when the chemicals that cause them run their course. If those feelings are our primary focus, we are then forced to find new ways to get *more* money or *more* respect, and inevitably turn to increasingly unhealthy sources to get our fix.

First coined the *hedonic treadmill* by psychologists Dr. Phillip Brickman and Dr. Donald T. Campbell, this progression of pleasure uses lots of energy but doesn't get us anywhere—except back where we started.[4] Einstein is attributed to defining insanity as doing the same thing over and over again and expecting different results, just like the pigeon that pecks a lever a million times in the hopes of a food pellet that will never come. Even though the rewards of our evolutionary goals are critical to the pursuit of our Ideal, pursuing those rewards blindly on the hedonic treadmill will lead to insanity.

What makes this situation particularly difficult in today's society is that we have a limitless number of levers that we can push to get the chemical rewards that we crave. If we don't get the bonding reinforcers that we need from our partner, for example, there is the option of turning to pornography. If our selfie post doesn't get enough likes, we can choose to pump ourselves up by posting bullying comments on another person's post, instead.

When the addiction escalates enough, the next step is often turning to manufactured drugs that simply inject the chemical directly into the bloodstream, rather than deal with the actions required to generate them internally. Indeed, every chemical addiction, including cigarettes, alcohol, and even heroin, can be traced back to our craving for dopamine and the other chemicals that make up our inner reward system.

Cocaine, for example, works by blocking dopamine from being reabsorbed into brain cells, creating a flood of the chemical that lingers to create a powerfully pleasurable experience. It's not the powder that the user pays for—it's the feeling that it creates through excess dopamine. Similarly, painkillers provide synthetic opiates that have the same effect as our internal reward system, but much more concentrated (the name endorphins comes from "endogenous morphine," or morphine that the body creates internally). Pharmaceutical companies push these pills to pad their bottom line, preventing people from setting up a more consistent internal reward system that would provide them with the same chemicals in a healthier, more sustainable dose. These types of corporations will always exist to manipulate our evolutionary needs in order to fulfill their own addiction to financial rewards. But we can do more to take back control of our lives, and help others in our lives do the same.

The Solution

The solution to the problem of the hedonic treadmill is not to get rid of your goals altogether. As we've seen to this point, goals are not only critical to the pursuit of your Ideal; they represent your identity, and you can self-select them to better align your current self with the future version of yourself that you wish to become. What's more, the powerful chemicals that make goal achievement feel good are a critical part of your total reward system—as long as you understand they are only one part.

The more we can manufacture our own joy from the right sources, the less we will feel the need to peck at unhealthy levers to get our fix. We can do this by filling the gaps between the obvious rewards of our goals with the subtle, continuous drip of dopamine that comes from knowing that we are on the right path toward our Ideal.

This is what the I GOT This framework is designed to facilitate, and it does this through the controllable Objectives and Tasks that I will introduce in the next two chapters. When you combine controllable effort with uncontrollable goals, you can experience the greatest reward of all—flow, which is the focus of Step 5.

Milestone Goal Reflection Questions

These reflection questions are designed to help you think about the lessons introduced in this chapter and begin brainstorming about how you could come up with your own personal Milestone Goals. For a step-by-step guide of how to follow the specific steps of the I GOT This framework, scan the QR code at the end of Chapter 1 or visit theideallife.com.

1. Using the role that you identified in Step 3, write down all of the goals that you have successfully achieved within that role over the past year. List every win you can think of, big or small.

2. Choose one of those wins and write down all of the things that needed to happen for that success to happen that were outside of your control.

3. Now, write for five minutes about the ways in which this success could have helped you accomplish the mission statement you created in Step 1.

Stress

The ◆ Ideal ········ Step 1: Identify Your Master Goal

Dream Goal ········ Step 2: Visualize (But Don't Fantasize)

Horizon Goal ········ Step 3: Outline the Story of Your Life

Milestone Goal ········ Step 4: Find the Sweet Spot of Success

Objectives ──── Step 5: Control the Controllables

Tasks ········ Step 6: Make Happiness a Habit

Joy

This ········ Step 7: Deliberately Flow

CHAPTER 6

Step 5: Control the Controllables

Objectives

"The trick is to surrender to the flow."

—"THE LIZARDS," PHISH

The first four steps of the I GOT This framework, which have focused on the "I" of the Ideal and the "G" of our major life Goals (broken down into Dream, Horizon, and Milestone Goals), have all been about planning for the future. The Ideal is the master goal that connects all of our life roles together and provides a sustainable source of dopamine pursuit. Dream, Horizon, and Milestone Goals represent the mid-level goals that create a clear (but uncontrollable) path toward the Ideal.

In Steps 5 and 6, I will introduce the next two levels of the I GOT This framework—Objectives and Tasks. Objectives are short-term outcomes that will put you in position to achieve the Milestone

Goal, and Tasks are the baby steps that lead to the habit formation that will make these outcomes possible. You can think of them as levers you can count on to provide a consistent reward whenever you make the effort to push on them, just like the pigeons who learned how to control their access to the food pellets.

What both of these elements have in common is that they are *controllable*, which is essential to sustaining a consistent reward source that can fend off addiction and keep you motivated to pursue your purpose. Along with Tasks, which we will look at in the next chapter, Objectives also fulfill all the criteria of a SMART goal—they are Specific, Measurable, Achievable, Relevant, and Time-Bound.

SMART Objectives & Tasks

Specific, Measurable, Achievable, Relevant, and Time-Bound

Choosing the Objectives that will lead to achieving a Milestone Goal is similar to the processes that we have used in selecting the framework elements we have already looked at. By starting with the goal in mind, you can then back into the present by considering what steps would lead to a successful outcome. For example, one person I coached in the I GOT This framework wanted to launch a blog. That seemed overwhelming to them at the time, but we were able to break that goal down into three controllable steps. First, they would research available blogging platforms and choose one of them. Then they would research and write one blog. Their final Objective was to launch and promote that blog using their existing social media accounts.

By focusing on each step, they were able to eventually accomplish their Milestone Goal. At first, it seemed too simple of a plan, but the energy released from those small wins carried over into a sustained motivation to keep writing and building on the platform that they had created.

The step-by-step process of the I GOT This framework uses a specific system that includes setting three sequential month-long Objectives that collectively lead to a three-month Milestone Goal, but you can implement the philosophy behind this framework any way you choose. The important part of this step is breaking a goal down into smaller chunks and making sure that their outcomes are fully within your control.

In this chapter, I'll go into more detail about why control is so important to our psyche, and how we can fine-tune the amount of control we have over our short-term Objectives to set us up for flow, the greatest reward of all.

The Circle of Control

In William B. Irvine's *A Guide to the Good Life: The Ancient Art of Stoic Joy*, he separates events into three categories called the trichotomy of control: those we can control, those we cannot control, and those we have some control, or influence, over.[1] There is a great visualization of this idea in Stephen R. Covey's *The 7 Habits of Highly Effective People*, in which he describes how all of the issues in the world that we are aware of, along with all of our personal goals, can be placed inside a "Circle of Concern."[2] Within that circle is a smaller circle encapsulating the things that we can actually influence through our actions; this is our "Circle of Influence."

The Trichotomy of Control

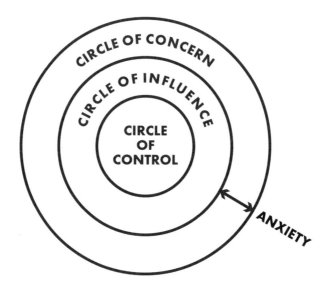

The gap that exists between our Circle of Influence and our Circle of Concern is the source of our anxieties; when we worry about something without being able to change it, this leads to stress. If we can shrink that gap (either by enlarging the Circle of Influence through skill development or shrinking the Circle of Concern by choosing not to think about things outside our influence), then we will naturally become happier by reducing the amount of unnecessary stress in our life.

Philosophers have long understood the importance of control in the pursuit of happiness. Aristotle taught that we can use our willpower to control the outcome of the deliberation between heart and mind; when we choose actions aligned with virtue, he said, we experience happiness. An important corollary to this, Aristotle emphasized, is that happiness comes not from the action itself but from the internal *decision* to act. This is what we have control over, not any external results that can be affected by the outside world.

Marcus Aurelius, the Stoic emperor of Rome, expanded on this idea in his journal *Meditations:* "The things you think about determine the quality of your mind," arguing that one can still find internal control even within the chaos of uncontrollable events.[3] Easy for an emperor to say, perhaps, who enjoyed the comforts of a curated external environment. But the Stoic slave, Epictetus, agreed, writing that "the chief task in life is simply this: to identify and separate matters so that I can say clearly to myself which are externals not under my control, and which have to do with choices I actually control."[4]

Psychologists have confirmed what these early philosophers already understood: whatever our life situations, evidence shows that humans tend to be happier when they choose to spend more time thinking about things within their control.

In the 1950s, the scientific studies supporting this idea were summarized within the psychologist Julian Rotter's "locus of control" theory, which differentiates people's worldviews by the extent to which they perceive the amount of control they exert in their lives. Those with an internal locus of control believe that the outcomes of their actions are contingent on what they do (they spend more time within their Circle of Influence), whereas people with an external locus of control tend to think that the things that happen to them are outside their personal influence (they spend more time within the outer part of their Circle of Concern).[5]

Countless research studies have been conducted on this dichotomy of perceived control, with consistent results revealing both the psychological and physical benefits that come with feeling like we are the masters of our domain. In general, those with an internal locus of control achieve more in school and work, act more independently, enjoy better health, and feel less depressed than those with an external locus of control.

These side effects are lasting. One long-term study of more than 7,500 people showed that children who had expressed an internal locus of control at age ten exhibited less obesity, lower blood pressure, and less distress at age thirty.[6]

Ultimately, the clearest demonstration of control over our life is through *self-control*. This is the willpower to control our responses to external events, and also the ability to manage our impulses and delay short-term gratification in exchange for longer-term rewards. Walter Mischel's famous "Marshmallow Experiment," originally conducted at Stanford University in the 1960s, tested children's self-control by having them sit by themselves in front of a single marshmallow, with the promise that they could have two if they delayed their impulse to eat before an adult returned to the room.[7]

Those children were then tracked throughout their lives, with the ones who had exhibited a higher level of self-control with the marshmallow reporting fewer developmental issues and higher SAT scores in high school. These results maintained remarkable consistency over several decades, with high correlations between self-control and overall metrics of professional success, including salary.

Locus of control theory has also been connected to the differences in mindset between optimists (internal locus) and pessimists (external locus). Psychologists refer to these differences as "explanatory styles," because they represent how a person explains the things that happen in the world around them.[8] Research shows that when goal outcomes are unsuccessful, those with a pessimistic explanatory style "attribute their poor performance to a basic lack of ability ('I can't do this') or to situations enduringly beyond their control ('There is nothing I can do about it')."[9] On the other hand, optimists "expect to have more control, to cope better with stressful events, and to enjoy better health."[10]

Over time, optimists tend to be happier than pessimists, with higher levels of oxytocin in their bloodstream. They also experience more success and less problems with their health. In addition to its relationship with less than optimal life outcomes, pessimism has another problem. Because pessimists tend to think that life is outside of their control, they will also think that being pessimistic is "just who they are," and there's nothing they can do to change it.

Carol Dweck calls this a "fixed mindset," because there's no room for personal development.[11] "I'm not good at math" and "I'm not athletic" are examples of a fixed mindset. A growth mindset, on the other hand, recognizes that there is always room for positive change when you focus on the things within your control. "I currently struggle with math" is a growth mindset statement and reflects an internal locus of control.

Just like math, we can also learn to become better at being optimistic about the control we have over our lives. In fact, being optimistic is something that we all have to learn from the time we are born. As babies, we are all born into a completely chaotic environment in which we depend on our parents for support. Little by little, we learn how to control that environment, learning how to walk, talk, feed ourselves, and eventually grow to become fully functioning adolescents and adults. The stress that we face along that journey constantly threatens to tip the scale back to a fixed mindset, but it is within our power to maintain an outlook of growth by continuing to create order out of the chaos around us.

Learning Optimism

Martin Seligman (a leading psychologist who would go on to found the field of positive psychology) developed a theory of "learned optimism," which says that we are all capable of developing an internal locus of control and experiencing the benefits that come along with the practice of a growth mindset.[12] But it took him a while to come to that conclusion. In fact, he originally became famous in his early career through a theory of learned *helplessness*, "which recognized that severe trauma can cause us to feel like we have no control over the world around us."[13] However, over the course of his career, Seligman observed that once we are able to observe the effects that our actions can have in influencing our environment, we can shift our locus of control back inside our Circle of Influence. Not only that, but this is the default way that we learn to navigate the world. The good news is that if you currently find yourself stuck in a pessimistic, external locus of control, there remains hope that you can escape that helpless state by learning how to better establish control over your life.

When we learn to stay centered in the things that we can control, and are able to align those actions with the pursuit of uncontrollable goals that we would like to achieve, we can accomplish things that we could have otherwise only dreamed about. Again, athletes are a great example of this in action. Let's consider the story of another swimmer, Katie Ledecky.

Excellence Can Feel Easy

On the morning of August 12, 2016, nineteen-year-old US swimmer Katie Ledecky woke up in the Olympic Village in Rio de Janeiro with a sore throat. The night before, she had stayed up well past midnight so that she could congratulate her roommate, Simone Manuel, who had just won an upset victory in the 100-meter freestyle. "She said I'm not going to sleep until I give you a hug," Manuel recounted of Ledecky. "That really meant a lot to me."[14]

Ledecky, who had always seemed to care more about the success of others than her own, was not without her own accolades. As the youngest American athlete in the 2012 London Summer Olympics, she had shocked the world with an upset win in the 800-meter freestyle, and now, four years later in Rio, she had already accomplished more than any other female swimmer on the national team. She began the 2016 Games anchoring the women's 4 × 100-meter freestyle relay, helping to win the silver medal and setting an American record in the process. In her second event, she set the world record in the 400-meter individual freestyle, followed by another gold medal performance in the 200-meter final. On August 10, she anchored another relay, this time in the 4 × 200 where she brought her team back from behind to win by nearly two seconds.

With four medals in the books, Ledecky had already made her mark on the competition, and her current state of fatigue was certainly understandable. But there was still one more race to go—the 800-meter freestyle. If she pulled off the victory, she would become the most successful female Olympic athlete in history, and the first female swimmer to win each of the 200-, 400-, and 800-meter freestyle events in nearly fifty years. But did she have enough left in the tank?

As Ledecky launched herself off of the starting block in Lane 4, her sense of self disappeared and she lost all perception of time. After the first 100 meters, she had already established a two-second lead. Fully immersed in the moment, she felt completely in control of her body as she propelled herself through the water. When she made the turn at the 500-meter point, she was able to see that the gap between her and the next swimmer had widened to nearly half the length of the pool. Even so, she had no sense of where her time stood against the world record and lowered her head to sprint for the last 15 meters without taking a single breath.[15] As she took off her goggles and turned to see her final time, her face broke out in a triumphant grin as she saw the clock display 8:04—another world record and over eleven seconds faster than the silver medalist. To put that into perspective, the time difference between the second- and third-place finishers was only 0.20 seconds.

When asked how her performance felt in a postrace interview, Ledecky said, "That felt really easy!"[16]

After her amazing 2016 performance, Katie began a full athletic scholarship to Stanford University, where she graduated with a bachelor of arts in psychology in December of 2020. As part of her curriculum, she would likely have learned about flow theory, a construct for optimal experience that helps explain how her dominating performance over the best swimmers in the world could feel so effortless and even transcendent, as if she had no direct connection to herself or her immediate environment. The paradox of flow is that this apparent lack of connection is the by-product of a complete demonstration of control.

Flow Theory

In 1990, Mihaly Csikszentmihalyi published his book, *Flow: The Psychology of Optimal Experience*, after a career spent researching the happiest moments of people's lives. What he found was that these experiences, while externally different for each unique individual, all provided the same internal feelings and characteristics as reported by the participants.

Csikszentmihalyi called the collective conditions meeting this criteria *flow*—"the state in which people are so involved in an activity that nothing else seems to matter"[17]—and his subsequent flow theory argued that a consistent facilitation of these states would "transform boring and meaningless lives into ones full of enjoyment."[18] Entering a flow state, he found, depends entirely on our ability to control our actions. "People who learn to control inner experience will be able to determine the quality of their lives," he wrote, "which is as close as any of us can come to being happy."[19]

When one enters flow, their sense of self disappears, their perception of the duration of time is altered (to seem either slower or faster than reality), and they feel a "deep but effortless involvement that removes from awareness the worries and frustrations of everyday life."[20]

The disruption of time seems to be a particularly strong identifier, such as when Katie Ledecky believed that she was significantly slower than her actual winning pace. Likewise, rookie football players entering the NFL often talk about how much "faster" the game seems to be at the pro level, only to later reveal that it "slowed back down."

Athletes are familiar with flow, which they sometimes call "getting into the zone," because of the way that sports naturally provide the necessary criteria to generate these states. But as Csikszentmihalyi found out, you don't have to be fully immersed in exercise to get into flow—it can be a purely mental activity, as well.

Have you ever been so consumed in reading a book that hours seemed to pass by like minutes? Or worked on a personal project that took so much of your concentration that none of your other worries or obligations seemed to exist? These are flow states, and research has confirmed that they make up the happiest moments of our lives. That's because when we enter into flow, all of the reward chemicals that our brain has to offer—including all four DOSE chemicals—dopamine, oxytocin, serotonin, and endorphins—are released simultaneously as a reward for achieving complete control in the pursuit of a meaningful goal.

Despite how happy flow makes us, we don't always consider flow-inducing activities to be the things that we most enjoy—partly because we aren't fully conscious of what's happening as we experience them. For example, Csikszentmihalyi identified that people are often much happier at work than they are while on vacation or resting at home on evenings and weekends, even though those same people predicted the opposite would be the case.[21]

As it turns out, even jobs we don't particularly like are more conducive to generating flow states—and therefore happiness—than the activities we typically choose to engage in when not working. If we could replicate these same conditions at home, Csikszentmihalyi argues, then not only would we be happier in general, but we could also reframe our perception of the role that work plays in our emotional lives.

Csikszentmihalyi's research identified several clear criteria that an activity must have in order to achieve flow. First, it requires the demonstration of a complete sense of control. Csikszentmihalyi describes flow as "the process of achieving happiness through control over one's inner life."[22] He explains, "we have all experienced times when, instead of being buffeted by anonymous forces, we do feel in control of our actions, masters of our own fate. This is what we mean by *optimal experience*."[23]

Next, a flow experience requires the pursuit of a clearly defined goal. That's why each one of the elements in the I GOT This framework represents a type of goal and why so much priority is placed on connecting these goals together into one prolonged path toward the Ideal.

The framework is designed to facilitate flow and to sustain those states throughout a lifetime of experience.

Finally, flow requires a full amount of focus. Focus is important because if you need to demonstrate a full sense of control, your mind can't be distracted by unrelated thoughts. This is why it is critical not to allow the hedonic treadmill that comes from focusing too much on goal achievement to distract you from the controllable actions required to get there. If you are thinking about the results, that means you aren't fully focused on the actions required to achieve them. The same goes for the temptations of instant gratification. Csikszentmihalyi writes that "the person who cannot resist food or alcohol, or whose mind is constantly focused on sex, is not free to direct his or her psychic energy."[24]

Finding focus is the hardest part of achieving flow. The truth is that we are constantly facing some form of distraction throughout our daily lives. Our attention is constantly being buffeted by the countless things that fill up our day. If you take a moment to pause and listen to your thoughts, you can hear the chaos of your internal dialogue.

Here's what mine is saying right now: *What time is it? We should probably get ready to go pick up the girls from school. What's that you said, stomach? You're hungry again? OK, I'll start thinking about where we can get some food. Ow! The lower back is acting up again—I better get the legs to stand up and walk around for a bit.*

With all of the things on our attention's to-do list, not to mention all of the unsolicited interruptions it has to deal with, the brain has developed the skills of a professional multitasker. In fact, neuroscientists have discovered that the attention can focus on up to seven different bits of information at one time—each for roughly one-eighteenth of a second.[25] That's why phone numbers are seven digits long: it's the maximum amount of information that our attention can hold together at one time for long enough to convert it into working memory. Aligning all of these bits around one connected idea is difficult. But when we are able to align our thoughts around the singular intention of a goal, we enter what Csikszentmihalyi calls the "flow channel."[26]

The Flow Channel

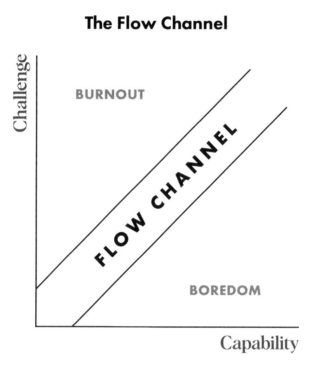

The flow channel occurs at the precise point where your skill level matches the challenges of an activity; in other words, it represents the point where your control is being fully tested. Think about the feeling you had the day you got your license and drove a car by yourself for the first time. The experience of learning how to drive with a permit, especially in the early days, was not particularly conducive to flow. In fact, it was downright stressful because the skill was still outside of your control and you depended on the support of a parent or instructor to guide you through the process. Csikszentmihalyi describes this as "the subjective condition that some call ontological anxiety, or existential dread"[27]; in other words, you were experiencing life outside of your Circle of Control. Over time, though, as you began to master those skills, you moved through progressive states of decreasing anxiety until you were finally ready to head out on your own. Finally, all alone, you were able to demonstrate those skills on the open road, and the odds are that this experience generated a blissful flow state.

The strength of emotions associated with an experience such as this allows us to recall it vividly. I remember my own first solo drive as if it were last year, navigating the country roads of Virginia's Goochland County to meet my parents for dinner. It was mid-evening, and there were just enough clouds in the sky to show off an amazing golden sunset. With the windows down, I could hear the loud chirping of a thousand crickets cheering me on as their song merged with the sounds of "Freebird" blaring from the speakers of my Jeep Cherokee Sport.

But that feeling didn't last for too many more drives, and odds are that the same experience happened to you. If someone had told you after your first driving experience that one day you would come to dread your daily commute, you would have thought they were crazy. But sure enough, over time, the skills involved in driving a car become so ingrained within us that we can do it without hardly paying attention at all. When this happens, we move out of the flow channel and into the zone of boredom beneath it.

Unfortunately, we typically only enter into the flow the first few times we perform at a new level of ability. Once we master a skill, we no longer need all of our focus to complete it, which leaves room for distracting thoughts (which, in the case of driving, results in extremely hazardous conditions as drivers allow their phones to capture their wandering attention). When we are bored, even though we still technically have control, we are not being called to fully *demonstrate* that control in the face of potential failure, and it is this demonstration of control that pleases our brains because it provides the recognition that we are moving forward in the pursuit of our goals.

Finding Flow

Katie Ledecky was able to enter the flow channel during her Olympic race because her performance included all the necessary criteria: it was completely in her control (nothing came between her and the water), it had a clearly defined goal (winning a gold medal), and it required a complete level of focus. At that perfect moment, she felt every positive brain chemical release as she focused on her swim stroke, and the result was something spectacular.

The feeling that Katie had as she finished her race is accessible to all of us on a regular basis. Unfortunately, it can also be very elusive to achieve. Life is constantly distracting us, and the hedonic treadmill can be difficult to avoid. The good news is that we can be more intentional than we might think in achieving the desirable outcomes of flow. In Step 6, we'll introduce another psychological theory related to peak performance called deliberate practice and reveal how the Tasks of the I GOT This framework can complete the quest for The Ideal Life by setting up a path of sustainable flow.

Objective Reflection Questions

These reflection questions are designed to help you think about the lessons introduced in this chapter and begin brainstorming about how you could come up with your own personal Objectives. For a step-by-step guide of how to follow the specific steps of the I GOT This framework, scan the QR code at the end of Chapter 1 or visit theideallife.com.

1. Using a Milestone Goal that you identified during Step 4, think of three controllable Objectives that would put you in a position to achieve that goal.
2. For each of those Objectives, write down the skills you think you need to successfully accomplish it.
3. Circle the skill that you are weakest in, and write down a plan that you can implement to improve that skill over the next few weeks.

The ◆ Ideal .... Step 1: Identify Your Master Goal

Stress

Dream Goal .... Step 2: Visualize (But Don't Fantasize)

Horizon Goal .... Step 3: Outline the Story of Your Life

Milestone Goal .... Step 4: Find the Sweet Spot of Success

Objectives .... Step 5: Control the Controllables

Tasks ——— **Step 6: Make Happiness a Habit**

Joy

This .... Step 7: Deliberately Flow

CHAPTER 7

Step 6: Make Happiness a Habit

Tasks

"It's no easy road, this struggle and strife."
—"THE SHOW OF LIFE," PHISH

The sixth step in the I GOT This framework is also the last one that requires effort on your part—you will see in the next chapter that the final step simply involves enjoying the rewards of all of your hard work. As the lowest-level goal in the chaordic funnel of your Ideal, the Task represents the final piece in the path toward purpose.

As you have learned by now, happiness is not an outcome. It is a habit. That's why the element of the Task in the I GOT This framework is designed with the latest science of habit development in mind. Because the Task is connected directly to the Ideal through the path of Objectives and Goals, your habits will become ingrained into the identity of the person you wish to become.

A Task is an activity that you can perform on a regular (preferably daily) basis. It meets all of the criteria of deliberate practice, which will be discussed in detail throughout this chapter. It is connected to the Objective, but where the Objective represents one-time stepping stones on the path to achieving the Milestone Goal, the Task is something that can be repeated forever as an identity-based habit.

For example, consider the Objectives from the last chapter related to a Milestone Goal of launching a successful blog. The Objectives were to research a blog topic, write the blog, and then promote it. The related Task for those Objectives was to write 1,000 words every day. As the client researched their blog topic, they began writing daily about thoughts inspired by their learnings. They then carried that practice into the writing of the blog itself.

But as that blog was finished and they moved onto promoting it, they continued to write about new blog ideas. Three months after they began the process and the Milestone Goal was complete, they moved onto deliberately practicing a different life role, but the habit remained. To this day, they continue to maintain a regular writing routine that has taken their skill set to a new level and has allowed them to consider new Horizon Goals that they had only dreamed about before.

This is part of the magic of the I GOT This framework—by focusing on simple steps that follow a clear path toward future goals, a level of mastery develops that gives you more control of your life and of your future. Marie Kondo started as a student in Tokyo, and now she is an internationally renowned expert. Muhammad Ali began boxing because his bike was stolen and he wanted to protect himself, and he became the heavyweight champion of the world. Michael

Phelps started swimming because his mom wanted an easier carpool process, and now he's known as the world's greatest athlete.

There is nothing inherently special about these people, other than their determination to make their happiness a habit. You and I can do the same. I used to be obese, and now I race triathlons. For over thirty years I had never written regularly, and now I am publishing a book. It does not take natural ability to achieve your goals—it just takes discipline. To prove my point, consider the story of Russell Wilson, the highest paid NFL superstar who nobody thought could ever play in the NFL.

Russell Wilson's Story

In high school, I shared the football field with Russell. Well, that might be a bit misleading … I *was* technically on the field, but I didn't exactly "play" with him. Okay, fine—I wasn't athletic enough to make any of our sports teams, so I had to satisfy my school's sports credit requirement by working the sideline chain crew for our football team's home games. But still, I did have a front-row seat to the "Russell Show": a complete, systematic domination of our competition, not only in the quarterback position but also as our defensive cornerback, and as our kickoff and punt returner. I remember walking toward the locker room with him one late afternoon when a coach called from across the field for the game ball that Russell still had in his hand; mid-stride, he casually flicked his wrist, and the football spiraled fifty yards through the air to land precisely in the bag the coach was holding open. At the time I couldn't help but believe that this kid was something really special, and I have followed his career closely ever since.

After winning the state championship in his senior year, Russell was featured in *Sports Illustrated*, and it seemed like there was no stopping his success. So I was dumbfounded when he wasn't heavily recruited by college football programs. How could any school not want him on their team? His statistics were impressive, they said, and he was clearly a winner at the high school level, but at five feet ten inches, he was just too short to play college ball.

What they didn't realize, however, was that Russell had been preparing for this argument since he began playing football at just four years old. His father knew that Russell's height would present future challenges, and so he taught him how to throw with an almost-locked elbow and a high-release point in order to compensate for his stature, and then practiced with him constantly.

Russell also excelled at baseball, and used this sport as a way to sneak into college football through the backdoor by convincing NC State's baseball team to allow him to also try out for football. Russell made the team, and in his first year took over the starting position from two taller quarterbacks.

In his third full season, he was named runner-up for the ACC's Player of the Year after leading the team to victory in the 2010 Champs Sports Bowl. That same year, Wilson was drafted by Major League Baseball's Colorado Rockies. He decided to participate in the Rockies' spring practice during the offseason at NC State, where he still had one year remaining of eligibility. But ultimately he decided that his dream was to play in the NFL, and so he returned for his final season of college football.

When he got back to campus, he found that his coach had decided to move on with another quarterback eight inches taller than Russell, despite the clear success that his star quarterback had delivered over the past three seasons. Wilson later recalled the conversation he had with his coach, Tom O'Brien: "He said, 'Listen son, you're never going to play in the National Football League. You're too small. There's no chance. You've got no shot. Give it up.'"[1]

But he didn't give up. Once again he was being told that he was too short, and again he found a way to press on. Securing a release from NC State that allowed him to transfer his playing eligibility to the University of Wisconsin, Russell found himself taking snaps behind the fourth-tallest offensive line in the country, with an average height of six feet five inches. Leading the Wisconsin Badgers to the 2012 Rose Bowl, Russell was able to show off the effectiveness of his high-release throwing mechanics to NFL scouts—but they still doubted. No matter what their eyes saw on the field, on paper he was still only five feet ten inches—which meant that he just wasn't tall enough to play in the big leagues.

On April 26, 2012, Russell Wilson sat through the first and second rounds of the NFL draft, watching as teams called the names of seventy-four other players, including five quarterbacks taller than himself. But then, with the seventy-fifth pick of the draft, Pete Carroll of the Seattle Seahawks decided to take a chance on the short kid from Richmond, Virginia. Carroll saw the determined work ethic beneath Wilson's physical shortcomings and decided to give him a shot as the third-string quarterback behind Matt Flynn and Tarvaris Jackson (both four inches taller than Russell). Once again, Wilson took advantage of his opportunity, and by the end of preseason he was named the starter.

In his first pro season, Wilson would break the rookie passer rating record, tie Peyton Manning's record for most touchdowns by a rookie, be selected for the Pro Bowl, and lead his team to a playoff victory. One year later he won the Super Bowl, the sport's greatest achievement. Then, in 2019, he signed a contract with the Seahawks that made him the highest paid player in the history of the NFL. The kid who was always too short had reached football's highest peak.

The Natural Ability Myth

When asked in an interview if he was surprised at his quick success at the pro level, Wilson replied, "I'm not surprised at all. I think, more than anything, it's my work ethic that has prepared me. I've done everything that I can to be the best that I can possibly be."[2] Another person not surprised by Russell's success would have been the psychologist Anders Ericsson (1947–2020), the "expert on experts" whose research focused on what the top performers in various fields shared in common. The results of this research, which he detailed in his book *Peak: Secrets from the New Science of Expertise*, were clear and intuitive, if not necessarily what you might want to hear. There is no "easy button" for success: in order to improve, you must practice at getting better. A lot.[3]

For example, in one of the many studies that Ericsson conducted, he found that the threshold for becoming an elite violinist was, on average, roughly 10,000 hours of practice.[4] This specific study became the inspiration for Malcolm Gladwell's popular "10,000 Hour Rule," which he introduced in his book *Outliers: The Story of Success*. In order to achieve mastery in a particular field, Gladwell wrote, you must practice its skills for at least 10,000 hours.[5] But Ericsson followed up Gladwell's 10,000 Hour Rule with a critical disclaimer: not *all* practice leads to improvement—it must be the *right* kind of practice. "The right sort of practice carried out over a sufficient period of time leads to improvement. Nothing else," Ericsson wrote.[6]

If you do the same thing over and over again for 10,000 hours, you are not going to grow. Ericsson calls that type of practice naive, because it seems like it would work, but it doesn't.[7] If you keep on practicing a bad habit over and over again, you will only get better at doing things the wrong way. Growth can only occur during practice where you push yourself out of your comfort zone in the development of new skills. Ericsson calls this *deliberate practice*,[8] and it represents the effective execution of a growth mindset that the I GOT This framework is designed to facilitate.

To understand the difference between naive and deliberate practice, think about how a child learns to tie their shoes. At first, it's really hard for them. I remember watching my kids trying to learn this—at first, even holding the shoelaces in their fingers was difficult. They would get frustrated and quit, and then come back and try again. Over time they became more comfortable moving the laces around, and eventually they learned how to tighten them and tie the knot.

Nobody is born with a natural ability to tie their shoes—it is a skill that we all must deliberately practice. After we learn the skill, though, it becomes firmly ingrained within our Circle of Control, and we can do it on auto-pilot. It transitions to *naive practice*, which isn't actually naive if you don't expect to improve at it. Instead, it is incredibly useful because it allows us to do things like brush our teeth, shampoo our hair, and even drive our car while devoting our attention to other topics. I refer to this instead as *comfortable* practice, which provides a platform on which we can push ourselves to new levels. When a deliberately practiced Task becomes an identity-based habit, it transitions into a comfortable practice that we can continue executing forever.

Ericsson found that top performers in all types of human endeavors—including sports, school, music, business, and even chess—learned how to build on their comfortable skills through a consistent application of deliberate practice. It is this execution of growth mindset, *not* natural ability, that always seemed to rise to the top.

As an example, Ericsson tells the story of Mozart, the musical prodigy and composer who could immediately identify the exact note played by any musical instrument. Known as "perfect pitch," this talent is extremely rare, occurring in only about one in 10,000 people. As such, it is what appears to be natural ability, or as Ericsson puts it, "a perfect example of an innate talent that a few lucky people are born with."[9]

Except that it's not. In 2014, the psychologist Ayako Sakakibara of the Ichionkai Music School in Tokyo published the results of a study in which twenty-four children, aged two to six years old and of varying musical experience, were given training in a very specific learning program called "chord identification method." A year later, the twenty-two children who had followed through with the entire study (two children dropped out) had *all* acquired perfect pitch![10] As other studies have replicated, virtually any child that *deliberately practices* can achieve this cognitive ability that was previously thought to be only genetically available to a small portion of the population.[11] This theory holds up with Mozart himself: as a young child, he received an unusual amount of classical training from his father who was himself a violinist, music teacher, and composer.

Not only is natural ability not required to succeed, Ericsson found, it can also get in the way. To prove his point, he uses the example of chess grandmasters. Chess is usually considered a game for intelligent people, and you might think that the best chess players in the world are also some of the smartest. But you would be wrong. Those who end up reaching the highest classification of chess grand-master actually tend to have a slightly *lower* than average IQ!

When players first start out playing chess, it is, in fact, the higher-IQ players that initially do well. However, their success leads them into a false sense of security in which they feel like they don't have to push themselves in their practice. The "average" players, however, who realize that they must put in hard work if they want to advance in the game that they love, learn earlier on how to deliberately practice the skills that lead to improved performance. Eventually, those skills pass the natural abilities of their "smarter" competitors, and their sustained practice habits allow them to maintain their advantage for the rest of their careers.

Ericsson was fascinated by this role of practice in performance and spent his career replicating these types of studies in many different types of environments, including athletics, music, and even business. Whether in sales or sports, the findings were always the same: over time, the deciding factor in performance was not natural ability but the consistent execution of deliberate practice.

These findings translate into a message of hope for all of us. Ericsson believed that we really can achieve most things that we set our minds to, as long as we pursue them in the right way. He had a vision of "a society of people who recognize that they can control their development and understand how to do it," and believed that "we need to get the message out: you can take charge of your own potential."[12]

In *Peak*, he goes so far as to say that "in the broadest sense this is a book about a fundamentally new way of thinking about human potential, one that suggests we have far more power than we ever realized to take control of our own lives."[13]

While the principles he uncovered were discovered through the study of elite performers, Ericsson found that "the principles themselves can be used by anyone who wants to improve at anything, even if just a little bit."[14] I'm living proof of this: by the time I turned twenty-seven, my athletic abilities had steadily declined from the not-so-high peaks of my grade school chain crew days. I was an overweight, sedentary smoker, and I never thought I could be anything different.

But within three years of implementing the I GOT This framework (which is carefully crafted to facilitate the deliberate practice of new skills aligned with the pursuit of your Ideal), I quit smoking, lost over eighty pounds, and completed an Ironman Triathlon, while simultaneously raising four children, earning a master's degree from Harvard and starting a business. If you start deliberately practicing your own Ideal, you can experience the same kind of results.

Mental Representations

The reason why deliberate practice is effective is because of its ability to control the creation of what Ericsson refers to as "mental representations."[15] Mental representations are the way that we learn new skills by being able to focus on more information at one time. The pursuit of our goals is limited by the seven slots of available space in our attention that I introduced in the previous chapter. If a task is too complex, we won't be able to do it.

I saw this failure firsthand when I helped my oldest daughter Lilly Grace learn how to ride a bike. She wasn't successful the first day that she tried, or the second, or the third, or the fourth. There were just too many bits of information that she was telling her brain to attend to: *Balance the body! Keep pedaling! Don't pedal backward! Don't put your feet down! Look out in front of you! Keep an eye out for obstacles! Watch out for cars! Have fun!*

Failure Occurs When We Need to Fit More Information Than Our Attention Can Hold

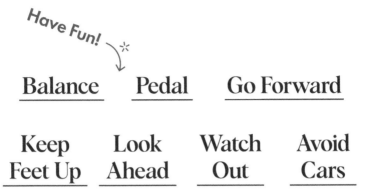

Because her goal of bike riding required information more complex than she was able to fit into her attention all at once, she felt uncomfortable and failed over and over again. But because she maintained full focus and kept trying, her brain eventually adapted.

The neural process for that adaptation is called neuroplasticity, and it works by connecting bits of information together by strengthening the connections between two or more brain cells. In other words, mental representations take two pieces of information and combine them through a common meaning. From that point on, this combined information can fit comfortably within just one slot of our available attention because the activation of one neuron immediately causes the entire chain to fire. Psychologists Bill Chase and Herban Simon refer to these neural clusters as "chunks," and they estimate that "by the time a chess player becomes a master, he or she has accumulated some fifty thousand [of them]."[16]

There are real physical changes involved with learning new skills. Wherever our brain stores these "chunks" of information, that part of the brain will physically grow. Brain scans of London taxi drivers, for example, have revealed that they possess an unusually large hippocampus, which is the brain system responsible for navigating our environments. Similar scans of mathematicians' brains tend to show larger than average gray matter in the inferior parietal lobule, which processes mathematical equations. In fact, an autopsy revealed that Albert Einstein's inferior parietal lobule was not only significantly larger than average, but it had also developed a distinct shape.

All of us have a vast collection of our own mental representations—most of which we passively learned throughout our childhood and adolescence. But we can also take control over the creation of new ones in the pursuit of a goal. To do this, we must be able to learn from our mistakes.

The Feedback of Failure

Being successful in a goal first requires failure. That's because whenever we fail at an activity, the feedback of our shortcomings is used by the brain to strengthen those neural connections during sleep, and the benefit of that growth can be seen the following day. Because activating one brain cell now automatically triggers others, additional information can now fit into just one slot in the brain's attention, which means you can now focus on more at once.

Every time Lilly Grace failed and got back on her bike, she was reinforcing new mental representations through small failures that made her better. Instead of *Balance the body!* and *Keep pedaling!* existing as two separate bits of information in her attention span, they became—*Balance the body and keep pedaling!*

Mental Representations Allow
for Skill Development

Have Fun!   **Balance**
and Pedal   Go Forward

Keep Feet Up   Look Ahead   Watch Out   Avoid Cars

For every person and for every skill, learning new mental representations through the feedback of failure is the pathway to improvement. The same process occurred for Russell Wilson when he practiced throwing like he was six inches taller, and for Katie Ledecky as she learned how to swim like a fish. It is also how I learned to conduct sales in business and manage people. Every knock on the door that led to rejection and every tough conversation that ended in frustration taught me how to be a little bit better in the way I communicated ideas and nurtured professional relationships.

Getting Out of Your Comfort Zone

Failing isn't fun, which is why many of us avoid the demands of deliberate practice. Not everyone wants to put in the hard work required to reshape their brain, but it's the only way to move forward in any area of self-improvement. However, deliberate practice isn't supposed to be overly difficult if it's done the right way. Rather, it aims for a level of stress high enough to facilitate learning but not so high that you burn out.

The benefits of this "Goldilocks Zone" of stress is one of the oldest discoveries in the field of psychology. In 1908, psychologists Robert Yerkes and John Dodson developed what would become known as the Yerkes–Dodson Law, which states that there is an inverse U-shaped relationship between stress and performance.[17] Yerkes and Dodson's research revealed that under-stressed subjects were not motivated to pursue their goals, while overly anxious individuals were too distracted by their stress to achieve success.

The Yerkes–Dodson Law

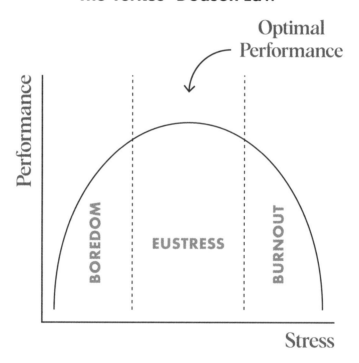

This "right amount of stress" was labeled *eustress* (using the Greek *-eu*, meaning good), described as "moderate or normal psychological stress interpreted as being beneficial for the experiencer."[18] On either side of this zone is *distress* (experienced as either boredom or burnout), which serves no purpose other than overwhelming your attention to the point where it disrupts your ability to optimally function.

This is where the final DOSE chemical comes into play: endorphins. Stress is experienced through the chemical cortisol, which makes us feel uncomfortable while simultaneously initating the fight-or-flight response systems that prepare us to deal with immediate physical threats. Part of this response is the release of endorphins, which are the body's natural opiate painkillers. This is the brain's way of preparing the body for the physical discomfort it thinks it is about to experience. However, the brain can't easily distinguish between physical and mental stress, which means that endorphins are also released when we experience the psychological stress that comes with getting out of our comfort zone. This is why pushing ourselves towards goal completion feels good, because we are seeing successful outcomes while simultaneously masking the discomfort with just the right "DOSE" of endorphins.

Ericsson's deliberate practice helps to achieve levels of eustress by taking an existing, comfortable skill and pushing it just beyond the comfort zone through the implementation of incrementally more difficult steps, which the Tasks of the I GOT This framework are designed to imitate. Through the small, incremental steps of deliberate practice, we can harness the energy of our stress and grow our mental representations one neural connection at a time. In this way stress is not an obstacle to experience joy, but rather a requirement.

Because it takes energy to create new pathways in our brains, we can only effectively execute deliberate practice for a short period of time before we need to rest. In fact, the second strongest correlation that Ericsson found among those who achieve mastery—besides time spent in deliberate practice—was time spent *sleeping*. Most elite performers, Ericsson found, slept more at night and took more naps during the day. In fact, they only deliberately practiced for about *one hour a day*, spending the rest of their time resting or *comfortably* practicing skills that they had already mastered.[19]

What's more, elite performers disliked the difficulty of deliberate practice just as much as lower-level performers; they just did it anyway.

As Michael Phelps puts it, "The difference between great and good [is that] the greats do things when they don't always want to. That's what makes them great."[20] The actual effort required to grow a mental representation by an additional neuron is the same no matter where you are in the path to mastery, just like a person running their first marathon is going to feel just as tired (probably more so, actually) than the person who finishes in first place. The difference is that top performers have been *consistently* adding to their skill set for many years and thousands of hours; over time, the same amount of effort produces a much greater outcome.

Just like lifting weights to grow muscle cells causes discomfort, so does wrestling with new skills. Both require failure to grow, and failure is never fun. It takes real energy, but it pays off in real results. The good news is that deliberate practice itself doesn't get harder over time—the results just get better.

I witnessed Lilly Grace's discomfort every time she deliberately practiced riding her bike. Before each attempt, I could see her stress response system firing on all cylinders, feeling threatened by the prospect of attempting to control this contraption that she did not yet know *how* to control. She was incredibly anxious, making me promise ten times that I wouldn't let go until she was ready. Every time she fell, she would complain that it was too hard and she "just didn't know how to do it" (her fixed mindset trying to conserve the energy required to try again). Some days she would give up, but other days she kept at it. And whenever she tried again, I would see something else click into place for her as she monitored the feedback of her failures and learned from her mistakes. She kept at it because I was there to act as a coach, a role which acts as another critical component of success.

The Importance of Having a Coach

The key difference between deliberate practice and other types of purposeful practice, Ericsson advised, is having a coach.[21] That's because a coach can make meaning out of our failures and teach us the right next skill to practice. Otherwise, we will waste time going through trial and error until we figure it out ourselves.

When Lilly Grace first got on the bike, I acted as her coach. First, I told her the basics—essentially, just how to sit on the bike and hold the handlebars while I pushed her down the sidewalk. As she became more comfortable with each step in the process, I would provide her with feedback on how she was doing and tell her one new thing to try out that I knew would push her into a new level of discomfort. By always catching her during her falls, I established a relatively safe environment that facilitated her full focus on the Task at hand without her having to worry about other external threats. Eventually, she had learned enough to ride on her own, and she didn't need me to guide her anymore.

Having a good coach to guide you in the pursuit of a goal is like trusting in navigation technology to get you where you want to go in the most efficient way possible. In Ericsson's opinion, finding the right guide is critical, but he also emphasized that they don't always have to be physically present—or even be alive.[22] The Stoic philosopher Seneca once advised his student to "Choose yourself a Cato," a reference to an influential Roman who had lived a generation prior.[23] Even though Cato was not physically present to instruct, the lessons that he had recorded were still helpful. This remains a useful strategy today. When Russell Wilson was a child, for example, he supplemented the lessons from his dad with videos of NFL icon Steve Young, whose style indirectly taught Russell new skills that he could use in his own practice.

In today's world of connected media, we can use the lessons from books, blogs, and YouTube videos to teach us new skills. With so much information at our fingertips it is easier than ever to learn about new topics that we are curious about, or to dive deeper into our existing passions. When we can connect with others who have the experience to guide us, we can avoid the pitfalls of naive practice and deliberately pursue our Ideal in the most efficient way possible. That's why at my company, The Ideal Life, we are creating a platform where coaches of all kinds can teach growth mindset to people in real-time virtual sessions as well as through courses that people can download and complete at their own pace.

Time to Execute

At this point, we have covered all of the steps of the I GOT This framework that require action on your part. To summarize, it all begins with the Ideal—a vision of the life you want to live and the person you wish to become. Then you set a long-term Dream Goal that brings focus to the Ideal, and a Horizon Goal that reveals the path it would take to get there. From then you set a short-term Milestone Goal, and establish a set of controllable Objectives that would put you in a position to achieve success. Finally, you create the conditions required to deliberately practice a Task that will lead to a comfortable habit that complements the efforts required to complete the Objectives.

Again, this is just a high-level overview of the framework's elements and why they work. You can use the principles covered in these chapters within your own personal approach to living into a growth mindset. If you are looking for more specific guidance, you can access the step-by-step guide for how to execute the I GOT This framework at the ideallife.com.

Now that you have put in the work of planning your goals, it is time to execute them. But first, it's important to understand the result that occurs when you implement the I GOT This framework. I call this reward Deliberate Flow, and it is the key to maximizing the benefits of the framework in all areas of your life.

 ## Task Reflection Questions

These reflection questions are designed to help you think about the lessons introduced in this chapter and begin brainstorming about how you could come up with your own personal Tasks. For a step-by-step guide of how to follow the specific steps of the I GOT This framework, scan the QR code at the end of Chapter 1 or visit theideallife.com.

1. Think about a habit that you want to work on in your life. Over the next seven days, maintain a tracking system that clearly shows when you succeeded and failed at keeping that habit.

2. At the end of the week, look back at the failures that you recorded. On a scale of 1–10, notice any trends (e.g., the failures occurred at the same time of day, or when you were the same person) and write those trends down.

3. Make a plan for how you will prepare for those trends over the following week, and track your results to notice any improvement.

The ◆ Ideal ---------- Step 1: Identify Your Master Goal

Stress

Dream Goal ---------- Step 2: Visualize (But Don't Fantasize)

Horizon Goal ---------- Step 3: Outline the Story of Your Life

Milestone Goal ---------- Step 4: Find the Sweet Spot of Success

Objectives ---------- Step 5: Control the Controllables

Tasks ---------- Step 6: Make Happiness a Habit

Joy

This ---------- Step 7: Deliberately Flow

CHAPTER 8

Step 7: Deliberately Flow

This

> "I see the future is less and less there
> and the past has vanished in the air."
> —"LIGHT," PHISH

The final component of the "I GOT This" framework is "This," which represents what happens when we unlock the energy of our inner reward systems through the systematic pursuit of Tasks and Objectives that are aligned with the Milestone, Horizon, and Dream Goals of our Ideal. It is the result of the chaordic funnel that converts the vision of who we wish to become into the reality of who we are becoming.

Throughout this book, I've emphasized the way that each element of the framework is connected to the evolutionary design of the human mind, which releases chemicals into our brains and bodies that motivate us to pursue a better version of ourselves. These chemicals, in turn, influence the way we feel in any given moment. Dopamine makes us feel motivated to pursue goals, oxytocin makes us feel connected to others, serotonin makes us feel happy and fulfilled, and endorphins give us a deep state of bliss.

The effectiveness of the I GOT This framework lies in its ability to help activate these chemicals by choosing deliberate thoughts and actions within a targeted goal in a specific life role. But the magic of the framework comes from how those chemicals tend to linger in the bloodstream for seconds, minutes, and even hours after they have been activated, which allows their positive effects to then impact every other area of your life. This is called the "spillover effect,"[1] and it is the mechanism through which the I GOT This framework leads to a joyful life.

The Spillover Effect

In general, the spillover effect can either work for you or against you. For example, think about the following two scenarios. First, consider a morning where everything goes wrong. You wake up late, have an argument with your partner over breakfast, and then catch every red light on your way to work. As you walk into the office you feel tired, angry, and annoyed, and you carry that attitude with you. You may be short with your coworkers as they greet you at the door, and your work will likely not be productive.

Now, consider how you would feel if things had gone better. You wake up feeling rested, enjoy a nice chat over breakfast, and have a smooth drive to work that gets you to the office ten minutes early. As you walk into the office you are feeling energized and friendly, and stop to chat with coworkers on your way to the desk. As you sit down you consider your goals for the day and get to work.

In both of the above scenarios, the way you entered the office was directly affected by the events that occurred before you got there.

More specifically, you were feeling the lingering effects of chemicals released by your earlier experiences. This is an extreme example of what happens to us constantly throughout every day. In any situation, our feelings are a combination of the demands of the present moment and the lingering effects of our immediate past. Understanding this, we can choose to take more control of our immediate future by being deliberate about our current mindset.

The I GOT This framework is designed to maximize the release of motivating, joyful chemicals that then linger and affect things unrelated to the framework itself—the "This" of everyday life. When you are consistently practicing the pursuit of purpose, you will realize that you have a confidence about your life that was missing before. When you implement the framework consistently, you will end up telling yourself, "I GOT This"—not just in regard to the goal you are pursuing, but to life itself.

For example, when I began using the I GOT This framework to lose weight, I was still regularly smoking cigarettes. I had tried to quit countless times before. It wasn't my desire that was different this time; it was the fact that I had created a new internal balance that set the stage for success. A couple weeks into my deliberate practice, I woke up one day and simply decided not to smoke again. That was eight years ago, and I still have not so much as puffed on a cigarette since. Because my craving for the chemicals that the nicotine and the habit provided was being filled in healthier ways, the motivation of my delibcrate flow gave me the energy I needed to change my life for good.

If you implement the I GOT This framework in your own life, you will start waking up with more energy and navigating the nuances of daily life with more control—not of your environment, but of the internal reactions that you have in response to that environment. Going into a big interview? You GOT This. Find yourself in a challenging conversation? You GOT This. Deciding whether or not to get off the couch and go to the gym? You GOT This!

The more instances of flow you can encounter, the more benefits you will receive from the spillover effect. That's because flow experiences correspond to a massive dump of virtually every reward chemical your brain has to offer. Although flow is an elusive state to enter, in this chapter I will reveal why the I GOT This framework is the best way to maximize the amount of time we spend "in the zone." The reason is explained by a new term that I have created called "deliberate flow."

Deliberate Flow

Deliberate flow is an explanation for how Anders Ericsson's deliberate practice theory and Mihaly Csikszentmihalyi's flow theory connect. Both of these psychologists studied the psychology of success from their own lens of perspective. For Ericsson, it was about the stress of pushing beyond one's current comfort zone through goal achievement. For Csikszentmihalyi, success was feeling happy and in control all the time. But when you look closely, there is a lot of overlap between their respective ideas.

First of all, deliberate practice and flow theory both share similar criteria. For example, they both have a clear path to goal achievement that requires specific tasks which demand both focus and feedback. The only area where they clearly diverge is in regard to one's comfort zone: in deliberate practice you must get just outside of this zone, while in flow your aim is to toe the line of that boundary. Unfortunately, simply because of this one apparent contradiction, they both considered the other's theories to be fundamentally flawed.

In her book titled *Grit: The Power of Passion and Perseverance*, psychologist Angela Duckworth details the disagreement between her two contemporaries. Ericsson, she explains, felt that pleasure and performance tended not to coexist. He was "skeptical that deliberate practice could ever feel as enjoyable as flow. In his view, 'skilled people' can sometimes experience highly enjoyable states ('flow' as described by Mihaly Csikszentmihalyi) during their performance. These states are, however, incompatible with deliberate practice."[2] Csikszentmihalyi, on the other hand, responded to that claim with his own subtle jab at Ericsson, saying that "researchers who study the development of talents have concluded that to learn any complex skill well takes about 10,000 hours of practice … and the practice can be very boring and unpleasant. While this state of affairs is all too often true, the consequences are by no means self-evident."[3]

Deliberate Practice vs. Flow

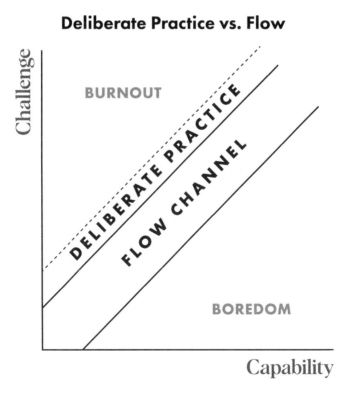

What's interesting about the conflict between these experts is not so much where they disagreed in their frameworks, as much as the fact that they acknowledged that both constructs are important processes in the lives of successful people. Ericsson grudgingly admitted that high performers do experience flow, and likewise Csikszentmihalyi conceded that practice "all too often" leads to success.[4] But if both appear throughout the course of improved performance, then how can they be completely incompatible?

This was the question that Duckworth posed to the two men when she brought them together for the only debate they ever engaged in over the course of their careers. If she could get them to speak directly to each other about the similarities of their theories, she thought, perhaps she could get them to hash out their differences and find the common ground that could help people to improve their lives.

As the two psychologists took the stage, they turned to face the audience … and then proceeded to ignore each other completely as they simply presented their own ideas to the crowd without directly acknowledging the other's points. After it was over, Duckworth confessed that she was disappointed. "Somehow, the dialogue I hoped would resolve this conundrum played out as two separate presentations—one on deliberate practice and the other on flow—spliced together. I still didn't have an answer to my question: Is expert performance a matter of arduous and not-so-fun-in-the-moment exertion, or can it be effortless and joyous?"[5]

After the debate, Duckworth got to work collecting her own data, which revealed that successful people *do more deliberate practice and experience more flow.* As she explains, "there's no contradiction here, for two reasons. First, deliberate practice is a behavior, and flow is an experience. Anders Ericsson is talking about what experts *do*; Mihaly Csikszentmihalyi is talking about how experts *feel*. Second, you don't have to be doing deliberate practice and experiencing flow at the same time. And, in fact, I think that for most experts, they rarely go together … In other words, deliberate practice is for preparation, and flow is for performance. The idea of years of challenge-exceeding-skill practice leading to moments of challenge-meeting-skill flow explains why elite performance can *look* so effortless; in a sense, it *is*."[6]

I can vividly remember where I was as I read Duckworth's personal opinion about the path to mastery. Like the epiphany I had when I picked up Covey's *7 Habits*, I felt that I was about to experience another turning point in my understanding of the human design. This would explain why Katie Ledecky's world-class trouncing of the best swimmers in the world "felt easy"; you can bet that the years of practice leading up to her performance were extremely hard. I had already seen the power of both deliberate practice and flow as a result of the I GOT This framework. I knew that the framework was effective, but I was eager to know *why*. What is it about pushing through discomfort that inevitably leads to happiness? Why does hard work often make life seem easier? I couldn't turn the pages fast enough in anticipation of Duckworth's conclusion. Unfortunately, much like Duckworth's own experience with Ericsson and Csikszentmihalyi, I was left a little disappointed.

"I can't tell you which of these accounts is accurate," she wrote, "and if I had to guess, I'd say there's some truth to both … as of now, there isn't enough research to say whether deliberate practice can be experienced as effortless flow. My guess is that deliberate practice can be deeply gratifying, but in a different way than flow. In other words, there are *different kinds* of positive experience: the thrill of getting better is one, and the ecstasy of performing at your best is another."[7] In essence, she was saying that for now, deliberate practice and flow would just have to agree to disagree.

But there's more to it than that! I exclaimed out loud to the book in my hands. It's not just that deliberate practice and flow *can* exist together—it is clear that they both *must* exist in order for either one to be sustainable. Deliberate practice and flow are not just compatible—they are *connected*. Unable to find a name for this connection in the literature, I chose to call it deliberate flow.

The Ideal Zone

In order to visualize how deliberate flow works, we can use the "flow channel" that Csikszentmihalyi used to delineate when one enters and exits the experience of a flow state. As we saw in Step 5, the flow channel exists where challenge and capability meet. When our capabilities do not meet the requirements of a challenge, we will experience anxiety because we cannot fully control the task at hand. It lies just outside of our Circle of Control, yet still inside the Circle of Influence—this is the channel where deliberate practice takes place.

Remember that when we fully focus on a goal just outside our control during deliberate practice, we are effectively telling our attention that it needs to fit eight bits of information into the seven slots that it has available. This creates resistance that we experience as eustress. If we push through that discomfort, then our brain uses that stressful energy to create a new mental representation that increases our skill level. As a result of deliberate practice, we can now perform the same task that we had previously failed at using only seven bits of information. Our attention is full, but not overly stressed—we are now fully in control. At the point this occurs, the eustress of deliberate practice transforms into the euphoria of flow.

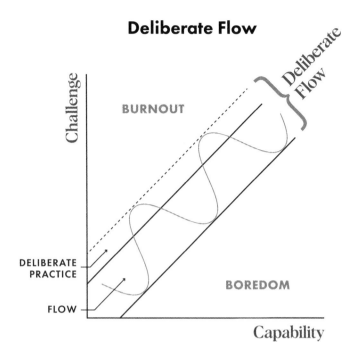

Deliberate Flow

I could see this progression of deliberate flow unfold as I watched Lilly Grace keep practicing on her bike. Little by little, she was able to pack more and more information into those seven slots of her attention, until finally she got to the point where she could stay up on her own. At that moment, her anxiety melted away, and she had the most joyous expression on her face as she disappeared around the corner of our block. For the first time, she felt like she was in control of her experience; she was in a state of flow.

It is at the point when our attention is fully focused on a goal *at the very edge of our comfort zone* that we enter into flow. For a moment in time, we feel completely in control of our environment in a way we have never experienced before, through the process of skill development in the pursuit of a goal. Our entire reward system is designed for this purpose, and it rewards us with a full DOSE of every chemical it has to offer—dopamine, oxytocin, serotonin, and endorphins. That's why flow feels so good, but unfortunately it doesn't last forever.

At some point, we allow a bit of unrelated information to enter our attention—perhaps a phone call or we get hungry—and we exit the flow channel. It would be nice if we could just hop right back in, but that usually doesn't work. The experience began at the point where we demonstrated the control of a new skill, but now that skill is just another part of our comfortable practice, even if just barely. If we want to experience flow again, we must push ourselves back out of our comfort zone in the pursuit of yet another *new* skill.

The pursuit of happiness, then, is just that—a pursuit. Sustainable joy is the result of a constant pursuit of flow that comes from consistently alternating between the productive eustress of deliberate practice and its fulfilling by-product of flow. Rather than just wait for flow experiences to occur, we can deliberately control them by staying inside the expanded channel that I call deliberate flow. It's a constant give-and-take; when we exit a flow state, we need to return to practice. But when our practice produces results, we must also allow ourselves to enjoy the flow.

The concept of deliberate flow connects the final piece to a puzzle already put together by the most preeminent psychologists of our era, who have themselves conducted the scientific research that confirms what the earliest philosophers discovered long ago. We are creatures of habit, always looking to create more order out of the chaos around us. The best way to do that is one step at a time, in the pursuit of a larger goal. The goal itself is not the purpose—it is the *pursuit* of the goal that matters. As Csikszentmihalyi himself puts it: "The purpose of flow is to keep on flowing, not looking for a peak or utopia but staying in the flow. It is not a moving up but a continuous flowing; you move up to keep the flow going."[8]

Sometimes it might feel like we are in flow during a mindless activity, such as watching TV or scrolling through social media, because our sense of time seems altered. But anxiety is not cured by trying to clear your mind of its thoughts; rather, it is harnessed by fully filling your focus with the intention to complete a specific goal-related task. True flow, and the psychological benefits that come from it, can only occur through the skill development that comes from the pursuit of a goal. On the other side of flow your brain has literally changed through the growth of new mental representations. You are a different person, and one step closer to the Ideal version of yourself.

Which brings us full circle in the I GOT This framework. It all started with the Ideal, a vision of a perfect life in which you have lived into each one of your seven life roles over the course of a lifetime. That Ideal was then used to create a series of Dream, Horizon, and Milestone Goals that brought that vision into focus, providing direction for a set of controllable Objectives and bite-sized Tasks that push you forward along a path of purpose. By starting with high-level goals and funneling them down a chaordic funnel into controllable next steps, the framework establishes the criteria required for deliberate practice, and thus sets the stage for a flow experience. And because the Ideal allows for each experience to be one step along a never-ending journey, those flow experiences can be sustained from one goal to the next.

The Discipline of Joy

As you can see, the I GOT This framework is not an "easy button" that makes life instantly turn into a piece of cake. In fact, it is the opposite—the only way for the framework to be effective is to periodically make life hard. And even then, there will still be times when you feel distress and can't seem to make sense of the pain in your life. Even with all of the benefits that the I GOT This framework has provided me in my own life, I still suffer from anxiety. I experience occasional panic attacks that leave me debilitated for days, and I experience burnout when I push myself too hard. But at the same time, I know that, on average, I have much more control over my stress than I would have without the intentional focus on a growth mindset that the I GOT This framework provides.

This is a journey that doesn't have a final destination—at least not in this lifetime. Every few months the framework requires switching from one life role to another, using the same Ideal to establish a new set of Goals, Objectives, and Tasks that keep your life balanced and joyful. This requires discipline, but that discipline unlocks a source of energy that makes you *want* to keep pushing yourself into new opportunities for flow. Jocko Willink, the retired US Navy SEAL officer and coauthor of the number one *New York Times* bestseller *Extreme Ownership: How U.S. Navy SEALs Lead and Win*, likes to repeat the mantra "discipline equals freedom." His social media accounts are full of images of his watch showing the ridiculously early time that he wakes to get in his morning workout. His belief is that when you create ordered discipline in your life, you free yourself to pursue the purpose that you were designed for.

The I GOT This framework helps you create this discipline in your life. By aligning your goals around the peak of the Ideal through the systematic planning of Dream, Horizon, and Milestone Goals and the execution of Objectives and Tasks, it will maximize the amount of time that you spend in a state of deliberate flow that exists between boredom and burnout. This is a journey that never ends. But that's OK because you can experience the joy of this journey every day. Eventually your Horizon Goals will become Milestone Goals, and you will realize more of your Dreams than you ever thought possible. But as long as you keep your personal Ideal in front of you, there will always be more to drive you forward. If you want to improve your life, if you want to harness your stress and convert it into productive joy, then I invite you to do so deliberately by identifying and pursuing your Ideal Life.

That Ideal, and the journey it takes to get there, looks different for all of us. We each have different goals that are unique to our own life. But we all share the same internal design, and that design rewards us for achieving our goals.

You don't need the specific steps of the I GOT This framework to experience deliberate flow, but you can be sure that the philosophy behind the framework can be found in every fulfilled life. If you have ever experienced the joy of pushing through hard work in the pursuit of a goal, then you have already experienced it for yourself. The I GOT This framework is just one way of describing a fundamental truth that exists for all of us.

Some people call their Ideal their "personal mission statement," such as the one that Covey helps readers write in *The 7 Habits*. Angela Duckworth calls it the "ultimate concern." She actually collaborated with Russell Wilson's NFL coach at the Seattle Seahawks, Pete Carroll, who calls his own personal approach a "life philosophy," but his definition of that term is strikingly similar to the Ideal. He told Duckworth that "I have learned that if you create a *vision* for yourself and stick with it, you can make amazing things happen in your life. My experience is that once you have done the work to create the clear vision, it is the *discipline* and *effort* to maintain that vision that can make it all come true."[9]

Perhaps one reason why Wilson and Carroll were so successful together in Seattle was because of Wilson's own lifelong pursuit of such an Ideal. When Russell was in middle school, he was asked "What's your favorite sport?" His reply: "Whatever's in season."[10]

Becoming the best football player was never his mission in life, which is precisely why he can still feel fulfilled even after signing the largest football contract in history. When asked what his purpose in life is, he responds, "I believe that God has given me a sense of leadership to be able to motivate other people, but also myself."[11] This is a goal that can continue to be deliberately practiced, even beyond his football career.

Likewise, Katie Ledecky's coach has described her own ultimate goal of perpetual improvement: "It's not winning an Olympic medal, it isn't setting a world record, it [isn't] becoming the best in the world. It's about setting goals and going after them."[12]

What goals are you going after? How do they tie into an overarching vision for your life? If you don't currently have a system for putting that plan together, the I GOT This framework can help. You can access a step-by-step guide on how to create one for yourself by visiting theideallife.com or through the QR code below, or you can sign up for one of our coach-led workshops where you can receive feedback and experience the joy of deliberate flow in a live group environment.

Regardless of where you are in your life, I hope that you are finishing this book with a renewed growth mindset in which you realize that you can control your inner joy. Don't be afraid to fail, because failure is the path to improvement. Stress is inevitable, but

the way in which we choose to harness that stress can be controlled. Never perfectly, but better and better every day. Take it one step at a time, and get ready to be amazed at how far that will take you. You GOT This!

Experience Joy

"Read the book!"

—"ICCULUS," PHISH

When I was in my senior year at Clemson University, our head football coach, Tommy Bowden, resigned mid-season due to the team's poor performance. He was temporarily replaced by one of his assistants, Dabo Swinney, which was a surprising pick because at that time Dabo was not second-in-command on the organization chart—he had never even served as a coordinator, the position that typically comes before becoming a head coach. In fact, several years earlier he wasn't even a coach at all—he had been selling real estate full time. However, he had become one of the team's best recruiters and our school's athletic director thought that Swinney would be the best choice to keep high school players who had committed to Clemson from considering going to another college.

It was just an interim title while the school conducted a formal search for a long-term hire, but Swinney knew that he had an opportunity to be considered for the permanent position. So for the rest of that season, Dabo set out on a mission to win the hearts and minds of the fanbase and convince the school's Board of Trustees that they should take a chance on him. As part of this campaign, Swinney invited the student body to one of the team's practices, and so my roommates and I went out to see what this new coach was all about.

I'll never forget meeting Coach Swinney for the first time. After an hour of letting us watch the team's normal drills, Dabo blew his whistle and gathered all the students around him as if it were a team meeting. I gathered with my other classmates and took a knee, ready to hear a pep talk about how well our team was going to perform and why we should support his efforts to become the long-term coach. But that's not what he said at all.

Instead, he spoke to us about *our* potential as students, and about how we could become the best versions of ourselves if we identified the type of life we wanted to have and then put in the hard work to get there. "Life isn't all about material success," he said. "It's about being a good person. If you practice this every day, then life will become what you make of it."

I was blown away. This man had been given a platform to sell his own agenda, and instead had used that space to do what he felt was more important: teaching us how to develop a growth mindset so that we could achieve our own success.

Clemson lost its first game under Coach Swinney, and just barely squeaked out a winning 4-3 record in the seven games left in the season. But despite the mediocre results, the school saw something special in Swinney's unique approach and gave him a chance to see what would come of it, naming him the official head coach of the Clemson football program.

Swinney immediately set to work aligning goals for his team that he knew would unlock energy within the players. He set his ideal vision for the team not on a number of national championships but on the development of young men into adults, saying that "You can win, win, win, but if you're not equipping young men to be great husbands and fathers, you lose."[1] Rather than use the number of wins as a metric of success toward that pursuit, he used graduation rates. "The goal of our program is graduating young men,"[2] he repeated over and over again to the press in response to questions about how he planned to improve the broken program he had inherited.

As he backed into the present from that future vision for his team, Swinney established a series of short-, medium-, and long-term goals that provided a clear path forward for his players. Goal number one, he said, was to win the first game of the season. After that, it was to win the division. Then the conference. Then the state championship, which was the annual game with Clemson's closest rival South Carolina. And finally, the last goal of each season was to "win the final game." Not win a national championship, because that depended on a decision made by a third-party panel of voters. Swinney knew that having a sense of control over achieving their goals would be important.

To address the specific controllable actions on the path to achieving these goals, Swinney hired the best football minds in the country to teach the players how to deliberately practice the right skills required to master their positions. He was able to do this by negotiating a smaller salary for himself (you read that right) so that he could use the extra funds to hire assistants that probably could have been head coaches at other schools. In 2012, the ratio of his salary to that of the combined coaching staff was the lowest of any head coach in all the major college football conferences. But he knew that having the right coach to teach the details of how to improve is critical to the pursuit of one's goals.

Finally, each year Swinney would institute a single-word mantra for the season. One year that word was "love," and another it was "joy." As the coaching staff repeated these mantras throughout their practices, meetings, and games, the players knew that the reason for their focused actions was so that they could achieve the goals on the path ahead of them, and that these goals were there so that they could become better men. In other words, they could see the connection between their Tasks and their Ideal, and this connection unlocked the energy that comes from being on the right path.

You can see the elements of the I GOT This framework at work in Swinney's methodology: identifying an abstract vision for the Ideal team, establishing a clear path of Goals that lead from the short term to the long term, and controlling the deliberate practice of the Objectives and Tasks that would maximize the chances of achieving those goals. If you have read the lessons from this book, you will not be surprised by the immediate and significant results that occurred.

In 2009, Swinney's first full season as head coach, Clemson won their first ever division title. They won again in 2011, this time also winning the overall conference. In 2015, they made it all the way to the National Championship game, and in 2016, they won the national title, the sport's highest achievement. Two years later, they won it again, this time becoming the first team in the history of college football to make it undefeated through fifteen games in one season. National pundits began referring to "Dabo's Dynasty," and after less than a decade of coaching he was already being considered in the list of the greatest of all time.

Swinney's life had not always been one of success. Growing up, he was surrounded by struggle. He witnessed his brother going into a coma for weeks following a serious car wreck when he was sixteen and watched the mental trauma of his recovery that would eventually lead to a life of alcoholism. His father was an alcoholic himself, which led to domestic violence and eventually divorce. After the split, Swinney and his mother were forced to stay in motels while he went to high school and she worked at a department store for $8 an hour.

But even with all of the challenges, Dabo stayed positive. He made honor roll at school and was accepted to the University of Alabama, where he walked onto the football team and eventually won a national championship as a wide receiver. Rather than lean into his personal success as an escape from the struggles of his childhood, he saw his achievements as an outcome of the path that he was continuing to follow. He invited his mom to come to campus and live in his apartment, even sharing a bed with her so that she would have a safe place to stay. As one of his teammates would say of the situation, Swinney's challenges were "part of who he is, and it's part of God's plan for him."[3]

Dabo likewise connected his journey to God's plan, believing that his successes only came as a product of his struggles. "If there's really hope in the future, then there's power in the present to deal with whatever mess you're dealing with in your life, to step through, to hang in there, to persevere, to continue to believe in something, and that's what my relationship with Christ did for me."[4]

This connection to God's plan showed up in the way that Dabo talked about his successes on the field, once his victories had given him a platform in the national spotlight. Just like he had used his interim position years earlier as a platform to teach the students how to become the best versions of themselves, he was doing it again on a global scale. This time, he had an even more important message to share—why we should want to become better in the first place.

In 2018, Swinney had chosen the word "joy" as the mantra for the team's deliberate practice. After winning the national championship that year, a reporter referenced this word in her postgame interview, asking, "Dabo, there are few coaches in any sport who show more joy than you do. How do you describe the joy of the moment?"

He responded, "Well, that's been my word all year, and I've tried to be intentional with that. For me, personally, joy comes from focusing on Jesus, others, and yourself."[5]

Swinney understood that joyful living comes from the deliberate practice of one's Ideal, and that the ultimate example of the "Ideal Life" was the one that Christ lived. When you follow Christ as the Lord of your life, it leads to the greatest success of all—the joy of God's love.

Dabo Swinney has achieved the highest level of success in his field, and he got there by leveraging the psychology of the human design. He used his goals as a direction to pursue a greater Ideal—in his case, as in mine, that Ideal is to imitate Christ. Not to be a perfect person, but a better one.

"Trust me, people that know me know I ain't perfect, but I do try to live my life in a way that hopefully can be pleasing to my Maker because I know I'm going to meet Him one day, and He's not going to pat me on the back and talk about how many wins I had or how many Coach of the Year trophies we got or how much money I made," Swinney said. "I really think He's going to hold me accountable to how I took advantage of the opportunity and the blessings that He gave me, the impact that I had on young people, the type of men that we develop through a game."[6]

Swinney has achieved success not by shoving his beliefs down people's throats but by living his beliefs in a way that attracts positive attention, and then using that attention as an opportunity to give glory to God. I am inspired by Swinney's example, because I also believe that the successes in my life are a direct result of God's grace. I have been broken, defeated, lost, and alone, but God's love for me has persevered. Now that this book has given me my own platform, I intend to use it the same way Swinney did, and give all glory to God.

God has given me a platform to discover and share insights into the ingenious design of His creation. In doing so, He has enabled me to help others navigate their own journey even as I continue the personal struggle to find my own way forward. Any success that I have had in my own life is due to the grace of God. Without the perfect Ideal exemplified by Christ to pick me up and guide me each day, I would have strayed from my path and remained addicted to the idols of my short-term goals. So, in conclusion, please allow me to provide you with what I believe to be the real reason why the principles behind the I GOT This framework are so effective, and the true purpose behind our human design.

The Real Reason Why the Framework Is Effective

This book has been all about *how* our bodies reward us for the perpetual pursuit of purpose, based on the inner systems of our physical design. The lessons of this book have been based on the highest output of academic thought, and their results have been documented not only in the stories from my own experience, but in the stories of some of the most successful and influential people from recent history. The principles behind I GOT This work, and I have done my best to explain how. If you are reading this afterword, then I have gotten your attention to the success that the framework can have in your life. Now, let me tell you the real reason *why* it works so well.

God created us as a reflection of His own character. Genesis 1:27 says that "God created mankind in His own image," and furthermore the apostle Paul says in Colossians 1:15, Jesus is "the image of the invisible God, the firstborn of all creation." This means we can look at the life that Jesus lived and learn the type of character that we should deliberately practice in our own life to better live into the intended purpose of our design.

Here are some examples of that type of character that we can use to guide us:

GOD IS PERFECT

That means He created us based on a perfect version of ourselves, and we can use this model as a guide to improve our imperfect reality. The more we can meditate on Jesus's life and use it as a guide for our own, the more we can understand the way that God intended us to live. When we act in ways that move us toward that model, we begin to flourish even in our broken humanity. We can do this by identifying an Ideal version of our life and then taking deliberate steps toward that vision.

GOD IS JOYFUL

That means He created us to be joyful. Our inner systems evolved to reward us with feelings of joy when our actions move us towards a better version of ourselves that more closely aligns with His perfection. The more our brains can see the path from our immediate Tasks to our controllable Objectives to a sequence of short-, medium-, and long-term Goals, and the connection between our long-term Goals and an Ideal version of who we can become, we will unlock the chemicals that combine to make us feel happy, motivated, and joyful.

GOD ESTABLISHES ORDER

God is the same *Logos* that the ancient Stoics used to describe the perfect order of the Universe, which we should try to align with to experience a greater sense of well-being. In the fourth Gospel, John specifically uses the Greek word *Logos* to describe Jesus, writing that "In the beginning was the Word" (John 1:1), which is the English translation for the original *Logos*. He was speaking directly to the powerful Stoics of his time, who represented the academic and scientific elite.

They had gotten it right, he was telling them, and they were talking about God. God created us to appreciate order within our own life. The more that we give in to the chaos of the world, the farther we stray away from our personal path toward a flourishing life. This leads to anxiety, which is the opposite of joy. By implementing a structured framework to develop our character, such as the I GOT This framework, we can better live in the order that we are designed to appreciate.

GOD CREATES

Much like philosophy can be used as an explanation of God's character, I believe that science is one path to understanding God's creation. Proverbs 4:5 says to "Get wisdom, get understanding; do not forget my words or turn away from them." I don't see the wisdom that comes from scientific pursuits as being at odds with Christianity, but rather a way of explaining it.

From that perspective, the theory of evolution can be seen as God's paintbrush for our own creation. Science teaches us that animals existed only after plants had facilitated a livable habitat, and that humans evolved after all the other animals. The Bible has been telling us that same story long before Charles Darwin came along. The creation story is one of order out of chaos, and when we create order out of the chaos in our own lives, we unlock the energy that God breathed into us at the moment of our creation.

GOD GIVES US FREE WILL

He had an intention for His creation and chose each step to take along the way. This means that He created us to do the same. Free will is the ability to make a decision after deliberating on potential choices. Because we have free will, that also means we have the ability to make imperfect choices. These imperfect choices take us away from the purpose of our design. God gave us the negative feelings of distress to let us know when we have wandered and to give us the energy to push into the things that are difficult but worthy of pursuit.

GOD GIVES US GUIDANCE

He has provided us with the mental representations we need to develop into the best possible version of ourselves. These instructions are given to us in the Bible. Jesus Christ is a living embodiment of those instructions, a perfect guide for the deliberate practice of a joyful life.

God's love for us is perfect, and He wants us to experience that love. But we are not perfect, and we never will be while in the chaos of this world. But in His grace He has created a way for us to be saved from our imperfections.

This entire book I've told you that you can use the Ideal as a direction towards a better version of yourself. But what if the Ideal wasn't just a direction—what if it actually was the destination, after all? What if you could experience the perfect outcome of an Ideal Life? You can—just not on your own. No matter how well you manage to stay on your own personal path of purpose, perfect joy is only possible through the salvation of Jesus's perfect sacrifice.

The good news is that if you have wandered well away from the type of person you know you should be, you have not given up the opportunity to experience everlasting joy. Jesus is Lord, and He has proven His love for us on the cross, and now He stands at our door and knocks. All we have to do is answer.

If you have not done so already, I invite you to open that door and invite Jesus into your life, believing that He is God's only Son, sacrificed on the cross for the forgiveness of your sins.

Thank you for the chance to tell you my story, and to share my faith in why we are designed to experience joy—its pleasure and its pain. Regardless of your personal beliefs or background, my hope is that you can use the scientific knowledge of our human design to harness your stress, discover your purpose, and achieve your goals in life. If the lessons in this book have helped you, please share it with a friend who might need help finding their own joy in life. Together, we've GOT this!

ACKNOWLEDGMENTS

For as long as I can remember, I've dreamed of being a writer. With this book, I feel more closely connected with that Ideal vision for my life than I ever have before. I still have a long way to go in my writing journey, but I am grateful for the joy that this step has unlocked. For the past three years I have alternated between ecstatic triumph at the way ideas have been able to come together, and literal tears as I stared at a page with no idea of how to translate my thoughts into written words. Along the way I have been supported by those who loved me, believed in me, and helped me make this idea into a reality, and this finished book is as much theirs as it is mine.

Again, and always, all of the glory goes to God. The ideas in this book, and the way they have been presented, are the result of God's work being done through my hand. I am both undeserving and eternally grateful for the way His grace has been made manifest in my life.

For the past decade I have existed as just one half of a greater whole, and I would be incomplete without the love and support that my wife Chelsea bestows upon me on a daily basis. No one else has seen the extent of my struggle—in this book, and in life—and she has been with me every step of the way. Thank you, Chelsea—I love you in every way imaginable.

The Ideal Life

To my children—Lilly Grace, Addison, Caroline, and Parker—you will never know what your existence has done for my life. You make me want to be a better person, and you give me the motivation to try harder every day. My hope is that you learn the joys of embracing a growth mindset and pursuing your dreams, and the discipline of focusing on the things that you can control. But regardless of what you do or where life takes you, know that I will always love you.

And to my parents, Jeff and Kay Congdon, and my brother, Whit, who have supported me from day one and have always encouraged me to pursue my dreams—thank you.

The list of the people who have influenced me could fill a whole separate book, but here I will try to list those who have most directly aided this project and the early stages of The Ideal Life. It is impossible to measure the impact of their support, and so I will list them alphabetically: Bryan Beam, Chuck Brueggemann, Elizabeth Buckley, Dr. Shelly Carson, Corey Coleman, Danny Conley, Sean Coughlin, Carl Dearing, Hutson Dodds, Father Ted Duvall, Nate Flores, Stephen Freeman, Shay Gregorie, Jena Gribble, Brianna Hill, Trey Hill, Brad Johnson, Keith Kopcsak, Oliver Marmol, Samantha Miller, Dave Newell, Dr. Stephanie Peabody, Harper Poe, Hannah Pniewski, Kyra Ross, Blake Shumate, Travis Smith, Lauren Steffes, Eric Thome, Hannah Todd, Jamie Tozzi, Karissa Tunis, Muge Wood, Bea Wray, Dr. Ayse Yemiscigil, Jono Young, and Christine Zmuda.

And finally, to you, the reader. Thank you for trusting me with your time and for your own grace in the imperfections of an early writer learning his craft. You are the hero of your own story, and I am grateful that you've brought me along for the ride.

<hr>

REFERENCES

INTRODUCTION

1   Chris Palmer, "Chris Palmer," February 2, 2023, in Armchair Expert, produced by Dax Shepard, Monica Padman, and Rob Holysz, https://armchairexpertpod.com/pods/chris-palmer.

2   Stephen R. Covey, The 7 Habits of Highly Effective People: Powerful Lessons in Personal Change, rev. ed. (New York: Free Press, 2004).

CHAPTER ONE

1   Aristotle, Nicomachean Ethics, trans. Terence Irwin, 3rd ed. (Indianapolis: Hackett Publishing Company, Inc., 2019).

2   Mihaly Csikszentmihalyi, Flow: The Psychology of Optimal Experience (New York: Harper Perennial Modern Classics, 2008), 34.

3   Angela Duckworth, Grit: The Power of Passion and Perseverance (New York: Scribner, 2016), 67.

4   KonMari, "How Marie Kondo Greets a Home," the official website of Marie Kondo, accessed March 30, 2023, https://konmari.com/how-to-greet-your-home/.

5   Csikszentmihalyi, 201.

CHAPTER TWO

1   CNN, "Phelps Wins Historic Eighth Gold Medal," August 18, 2008, http://edition.cnn.com/2008/SPORT/08/17/phelps.history.eight.golds/.

2   Eun Kyung Kim, "Michael Phelps Announces Retirement on TODAY: 'This Time I Mean It,'" TODAY, August 15, 2016, https://www.today.com/news/michael-phelps-announces-retirement-today-show-time-i-mean-it-t101844.

3   The Weight of Gold, directed by Brett Rapkin (HBO, 2020).

4   "Olympedia—Olympians Who Committed Suicide," Olympedia, accessed April 3, 2023, https://www.olympedia.org/lists/55/manual.

5   The Weight of Gold.

6   Ibid.

7   Buzz Aldrin and Ken Abraham, Magnificent Desolation: The Long Journey Home from the Moon, reprint ed. (New York: Three Rivers Press, 2010), 80.

8   The Weight of Gold.

9   "Definition of Purpose—Google Search," accessed April 3, 2023, https://www.google.com/search?q=definition+of+purpose.

10   Kenneth E. Vail et al., "When Death Is Good for Life: Considering the Positive Trajectories of Terror Management," Personality and Social Psychology Review: An Official Journal of the Society for Personality and Social Psychology, Inc 16, no. 4 (November 2012): 303–29.

11   Marcus Aurelius, Meditations: A New Translation, trans. Gregory Hays (Random House Publishing Group, 2003), 2.11.1.

12   Lucius Annaeus Seneca, Letters from a Stoic, trans. Robin Campbell (Harmondsworth: Penguin Books, 1964).

13   Mihaly Csikszentmihalyi, Flow: The Psychology of Optimal Experience, 1st ed. (New York: Harper Perennial Modern Classics, 2008), 9.

14   "FAQ," Angela Duckworth, accessed June 12, 2023, http://Angela-Duckworth.com/.

15   "FAQ," Angela Duckworth, accessed June 12, 2023, http://Angela-Duckworth.com/.

16   Jim Rohn, "Challenges to Succeed", 1981, 1:31, https://www.youtube.com/watch?v=NYgyxvYJ3VA&t=6s.

CHAPTER THREE

1   Heather Barry Kappes and Gabriele Oettingen, "Positive Fantasies about Idealized Futures Sap Energy," Journal of Experimental Social Psychology 47, no. 4 (July 1, 2011): 719–29.

2   Ibid.

3   As summarized by Angela Duckworth in Grit: The Power of Passion and Perseverance, 1st ed. (New York: Scribner, 2016), 65.

4   Gabriele Oettingen, Rethinking Positive Thinking: Inside the New Science of Motivation (New York: Current, 2014).

5   "What Oprah Learned from Jim Carrey." Oprah's Life Class, October 12, 2011. https://www.oprah.com/oprahs-lifeclass/what-oprah-learned-from-jim-carrey-video.

6   "Seven Down: Phelps Narrowly Grabs Gold in 100 Fly," ESPN.com, August 16, 2008, https://www.espn.com/olympics/summer08/swimming/news/story?id=3537831.

7   "Seven Down: Phelps Narrowly Grabs Gold in 100 Fly," ESPN.com, August 16, 2008, https://www.espn.com/olympics/summer08/swimming/news/story?id=3537831.

8   Carol S. Dweck, Mindset: The New Psychology of Success (New York: Random House, 2006), 84.

9   Andrew Anthony, "Muhammad Ali: Rebel, Showman and the Lord of the Ring," The Guardian, March 6, 2016, https://www.theguardian.com/sport/2016/mar/06/profile-muhammad-ali-boxing-i-am-greatest-exhibition.

10   David Remnick, King of the World: Muhammad Ali and the Rise of an American Hero, 1st ed. (New York: Random House, 1998), 93.

11   Ibid., 119.

12   Ibid., 175-6.

13   Oettingen, 2014.

14   Gabriele Oettingen, "WOOP My Life," WOOP My Life, accessed July 10, 2023, https://woopmylife.org/en/home.

15   "Seven Down: Phelps Narrowly Grabs Gold in 100 Fly," ESPN.com, August 16, 2008, https://www.espn.com/olympics/summer08/swimming/news/story?id=3537831.

16   Carol S. Dweck, Mindset: The New Psychology of Success (New York: Random House, 2006), 84.

17   Andrew Anthony, "Muhammad Ali: Rebel, Showman and the Lord of the Ring," The Guardian, March 6, 2016, https://www.theguardian.com/sport/2016/mar/06/profile-muhammad-ali-boxing-i-am-greatest-exhibition.

18   David Remnick, King of the World: Muhammad Ali and the Rise of an American Hero, 1st ed. (New York: Random House, 1998), 93.

19   Ibid., 119.

20   Ibid., 175-6.

CHAPTER FOUR

1   Jerome S. Bruner and Cecile C. Goodman, "Value and Need as Organizing Factors in Perception," The Journal of Abnormal and Social Psychology 42 (1947): 33–44.

2   Elissar Andari et al., "Promoting Social Behavior with Oxytocin in High-Functioning Autism Spectrum Disorders," Proceedings of the National Academy of Sciences of the United States of America 107, no. 9 (March 2, 2010): 4389–94.

3   See, for example:

Lisa F. Berkman, "The Role of Social Relations in Health Promotion," Psychosomatic Medicine 57, no. 3 (1995): 245–54.

Julianne Holt-Lunstad, Timothy B. Smith, and J. Bradley Layton, "Social Relationships and Mortality Risk: A Meta-Analytic Review," PLOS Medicine 7, no. 7 (July 27, 2010): e1000316.

Jolanda Jetten et al., "Having a Lot of a Good Thing: Multiple Important Group Memberships as a Source of Self-Esteem," PLoS ONE 10, no. 5 (May 27, 2015).

Maija Reblin and Bert N. Uchino, "Social and Emotional Support and Its Implication for Health," Current Opinion in Psychiatry 21, no. 2 (March 2008): 201–05.

Bert N. Uchino, "Understanding the Links Between Social Support and Physical Health: A Life-Span Perspective With Emphasis on the Separability of Perceived and Received Support," Perspectives on Psychological Science: A Journal of the Association for Psychological Science 4, no. 3 (May 2009): 236–55.

4   Abraham H. Maslow, "A Theory of Human Motivation," Psychological Review 50 (1943): 370–96.

5   "Definition of Faith—Google Search," accessed May 30, 2023, https://www.google.com/search?q=definition+of+faith.

6   Maslow.

7   Michael A. Ferguson et al., "Reward, Salience, and Attentional Networks Are Activated by Religious Experience in Devout Mormons," Social Neuroscience 13, no. 1 (January 2, 2018): 104–16.

8   Vilfredo Pareto, Manual of Political Economy, ed. Alfred N. Page, trans. Ann S. Schwier (New York: A.M. Kelley, 1971).

CHAPTER FIVE

1   Fred B. Bryant and Joseph Veroff, Savoring: A New Model of Positive Experience, Savoring: A New Model of Positive Experience (Mahwah: Lawrence Erlbaum Associates Publishers, 2007).

2   B. F. Skinner, "'Superstition' in the Pigeon," Journal of Experimental Psychology 38 (1948): 168–72.

3   See, for example:

Andrew Churchill, Jamie A. Taylor, and Royston Parkes, "The Creation of a Superstitious Belief Regarding Putters in a Laboratory-Based Golfing Task," International Journal of Sport and Exercise Psychology 13, no. 4 (2015): 335–43.

Oren Griffiths et al., "Superstition Predicts Perception of Illusory Control," British Journal of Psychology 110, no. 3 (2019): 499–518.

Yusuke Hayashi and James G. Modico, "Effect of Response-Independent Delivery of Positive and Negative Reinforcers on the Development of Superstitious Behavior and Belief in Humans," Behavior Analysis: Research and Practice 19, no. 4 (2019): 327–42.

Eric J. Hamerman and Gita V. Johar, "Conditioned Superstition: Desire for Control and Consumer Brand Preferences," Journal of Consumer Research 40, no. 3 (2013): 428–43.

Jeffrey Rudski, "Competition, Superstition and the Illusion of Control," Current Psychology: A Journal for Diverse Perspectives on Diverse Psychological Issues 20, no. 1 (2001): 68–84.

4   Brickman Phillip and Donald T. Campbell, "Hedonic Relativism and Planning the Good Society," in Adaptation-Level Theory, ed. Mortimer Herbert Appley (New York: Academic Press, 1971), 287–305.

CHAPTER SIX

1   William B. Irvine, A Guide to the Good Life: The Ancient Art of Stoic Joy (Oxford; New York: Oxford University Press, 2008).

2   Stephen R. Covey, The 7 Habits of Highly Effective People: Powerful Lessons in Personal Change, rev. ed. (New York: Free Press, 2004).

3   Marcus Aurelius, Meditations: A New Translation, trans. Gregory Hays, First American PB Edition (New York, NY: Random House Publishing Group, 2003)

4   Epictetus, Discourses, 2.5.4-5, as quoted in Ryan Holiday and Stephen Hanselman, The Daily Stoic: 366 Meditations on Wisdom, Perseverance, and the Art of Living (New York: Penguin, 2016).

5   Julian B. Rotter, "Generalized Expectancies for Internal versus External Control of Reinforcement," Psychological Monographs: General and Applied 80, no. 1 (1966): 1–28.

6   Catharine R. Gale, G. David Batty, and Ian J. Deary, "Locus of Control at Age 10 Years and Health Outcomes and Behaviors at Age 30 Years: The 1970 British Cohort Study," Psychosomatic Medicine 70, no. 4 (May 2008): 397–403.

7   Walter Mischel and Ebbe B. Ebbesen, "Attention in Delay of Gratification," Journal of Personality and Social Psychology 16 (1970): 329–37.

8   Christopher Peterson and Martin E. Seligman, "Explanatory Style and Illness," Journal of Personality 55 (1987): 237–65.

9   David G. Myers and C. Nathan DeWall, Exploring Psychology, 10th ed. (New York: Worth Publishers, 2016), 422.

10   Ibid.

11   Carol S. Dweck, Mindset: The New Psychology of Success (New York: Random House, 2006).

12   Martin E. P. Seligman, Learned Optimism: How to Change Your Mind and Your Life (New York: Knopf, 1990).

13   Martin E. P. Seligman, "Learned Helplessness," Annual Review of Medicine 23, no. 1 (1972): 407–12.

14   Karen Crouse, "Katie Ledecky Smashes World Record in the 800-Meter Freestyle," The New York Times, August 13, 2016, sec. Sports.

15   This description of Ledecky's thoughts and feelings are not from a first-hand account, but rather are my interpretation of what her mental processes must have been based on an understanding of flow theory, which will be a main focus of this chapter.

16 Coleman Hodges, "Katie Ledecky on Going 8:10 in Prelims: "That Felt Really Easy" (Video)," SwimSwam, July 1, 2016, https://swimswam.com/ katie-ledecky-going-810-prelimsthat-felt-really-easy-video/.

17 Mihaly Csikszentmihalyi, Flow: The Psychology of Optimal Experience, 1st ed. (New York: Harper Perennial Modern Classics, 2008), 4.

18 Ibid., xi.

19 Ibid., 2.

20 Ibid., 49.

21 Ibid., 143–62.

22 Ibid, 6.

23 Ibid., 3.

24 Ibid., 18.

25 George A. Miller, "The Magical Number Seven, Plus or Minus Two: Some Limits on Our Capacity for Processing Information," Psychological Review 63 (1956): 81–97.

26 Csikszentmihalyi.

27 Ibid., 12.

CHAPTER SEVEN

1 "Russell Wilson Takes Jab at NC State; Great Lesson Learned," AP News, May 15, 2016, https://apnews.com/ article/-----46db3f3c5cd946a6acb5c12e4fbfadb0.

2 Avinash Kunnath, "Russell Wilson Reacts To Being Named Starter," SB Nation Seattle, August 29, 2012, https://seattle.sbnation. com/2012/8/29/3277584/russell-wilson-seahawks-pete-carroll.

3 Anders Ericsson, Peak: Secrets from the New Science of Expertise (Boston: Houghton Mifflin Harcourt, 2016).

4 Ibid.

5   Malcolm Gladwell, Outliers: The Story of Success (Penguin UK, 2008).

6   Ericsson, xxi.

7   Ibid., 14.

8   Ibid.

9   Ibid., xiii.

10   Ayako Sakakibara, "A Longitudinal Study of the Process of Acquiring Absolute Pitch: A Practical Report of Training with the 'Chord Identification Method,'" Psychology of Music 42, no. 1 (January 1, 2014): 86–111.

11   See, for example:

       Angela Lee Duckworth et al., "Deliberate Practice Spells Success: Why Grittier Competitors Triumph at the National Spelling Bee," Social Psychological and Personality Science 2, no. 2 (March 1, 2011): 174–81.

       K. Anders Ericsson, Kiruthiga Nandagopal, and Roy W. Roring, "Toward a Science of Exceptional Achievement," Annals of the New York Academy of Sciences 1172, no. 1 (2009): 199–217.

       Erno Lehtinen et al., "Cultivating Mathematical Skills: From Drill-and-Practice to Deliberate Practice," ZDM 49, no. 4 (August 1, 2017): 625–36.

12   Ericsson, 259.

13   Ibid., xix.

14   Ibid., xxiii.

15   Ibid., 50.

16   Ibid, 57.

17   Robert M. Yerkes and John D. Dodson, "The Relation of Strength of Stimulus to Rapidity of Habit-Formation," Journal of Comparative Neurology and Psychology 18, no. 5 (1908): 459–82.

18 Tristan Williams, "Eustress: Definition, Causes, & Characteristics," The Berkeley Well-Being Institute, accessed June 12, 2023, https://www.berkeleywellbeing.com/eustress.html.

19 Ericsson.

20 Riley Overend, "What Did Michael Phelps Tell Alabama Football Players?," SwimSwam, January 16, 2023, https://swimswam.com/what-did-michael-phelps-tell-alabama-football-players/.

21 Ericsson.

22 Ibid.

23 Lucius Annaeus Seneca, Letters from a Stoic, trans. Robin Campbell, reprint ed. (Harmondsworth: Penguin Books, 1969).

CHAPTER EIGHT

1 Marianne Spoon, "Scientists Pinpoint Area of the Brain That Regulates Emotional Spillover," University of Wisconsin-Madison, June 19, 2017, https://news.wisc.edu/scientists-pinpoint-area-of-the-brain-that-regulates-emotional-spillover/.

2 Angela Duckworth, Grit: The Power of Passion and Perseverance, 1st ed. (New York: Scribner, 2016), 129.

3 Ibid.

4 Ibid.

5 Ibid., 130.

6 Ibid., 131.

7 Ibid., 137.

8 Mihaly Csikszentmihalyi, Flow: The Psychology of Optimal Experience, 1st edition (New York: Harper Perennial Modern Classics, 2008), 54.

9 Duckworth, 261.

10 Weldon Bradshaw, "Russell Wilson, the Early Years," Collegiate School, February 1, 2014, https://www.collegiate-va.org/news-detail?pk=715534.

11   Kate Fagan, "Russell Wilson's Kindness Leaves
      Mark," ESPN, January 30, 2014, https://www.espn.
      com/espnw/news-commentary/article/10375235/
      espnw-touch-kindness-seattle-seahawks-quarterback-russell-wilson.

12   "Ledecky Finishes with a Flourish, Gold," Northwest Arkansas
      Democrat Gazette, August 13, 2016, https://www.nwaonline.com/
      news/2016/aug/13/ledecky-finishes-with-a-flourish-gold-2/.

AFTERWORD

1   Joshua Cooley, "FCA Magazine Blog Page," Fellowship of
      Christian Athletes, February 28, 2017, https://www.fca.org/
      magazine-story/2017/02/28/only-god-can-do-this?utm_
      source=pressrelease&utm_medium=link&utm_content=17dabopr.

2   "Dabo Swinney on NIL: 'The Goal of Our Program Is Graduating
      Young Men,'" Clemson Sports Talk, July 23, 2021, https://clem-
      sonsportstalk.com/s/7135/dabo-swinney-on-nil-the-goal-of-our-
      program-is-graduating-young-men.

3   Mark Schlabach, "Dabo Swinney Overcame Pain
      and Poverty to Be on the Cusp of History," ABC
      News, January 7, 2016, https://abcnews.go.com/Sports/
      dabo-swinney-overcame-pain-poverty-cusp-history/
      story?id=36146292.

4   Zach Lentz, "Dabo Swinney: Relationship with Christ Was a 'Game
      Changer,'" Sports Illustrated, May 5, 2022, https://www.si.com/
      college/clemson/football/clemson-tigers-hc-dabo-swinney-relation-
      ship-with-christ-was-a-game-changer.

5   Zach Lentz, "Swinney Found Joy in the Moment--
      Not the Accomplish," Sports Illustrated, April 16,
      2019, https://www.si.com/college/clemson/football/
      swinney-found-joy-in-the-moment-not-the-accomplish.

6   Lentz.